# How to *Get Over It* in *30 Days!* Part II

## Daily Messages to Inspire and Empower you!

*The Empowerment Series*
## Adair f. White-johnson, Ph.D.

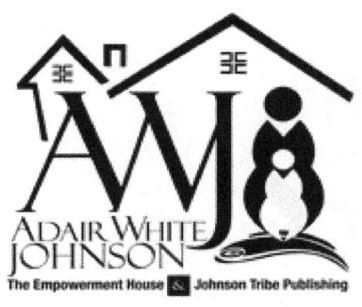

*How to Get Over It in 30 Days Part II*

Published by Johnson Tribe Publishing, LLC
Atlanta, GA

Copyright © 2014 by Adair f. White-johnson, Ph.D.
All rights reserved, including the express right to reproduce this book or portions thereof in any form whatsoever whether now known or hereinafter developed. For information address Johnson Tribe Publishing, P.O. Box 1587 Powder Springs, Georgia 30127.

Johnson Tribe Publishing materials may be purchased for education, business, or promotional use. Author is also available for speaking engagements. For information please contact us at (888) 400-7302, email us at johnsontribepublishing@johnsontribepublishing.com or visit us at www.johnsontribepublishing.com

The following story is inspired by actual events. However, the names have been changed to protect the privacy of those involved.

Manufactured in the United States of America

10  9  8  7  6  5  4  3  2  1

FIRST EDITION – December 2014
Creative Direction: Adair F. White-johnson, Ph.D.
Graphic Design: Stacey Bowers, August Pride, LLC
Book Design: DZine by Kellie

Library of Congress Catalog Card Number:

ISBN-13: 978-0989673365
ISBN-10: 0989673367

USA $12.95
Canada $15.50

*How to Get Over It in 30 Days Part II*

## DEDICATION

This one is for my Daddy, Paul Anthony White. I love you, and you still are the "wind beneath my wings" as I live each day of my life.
Thank you for this gift of touching a soul through the written word.

*Dr. Adair f. White-johnson*

# *Introduction*

"Get Over It!" means just to let things go that do not serve a positive purpose in your life. It means that you should do everything from the core of your existence... not holding back and sucking in the final morsel of air to exhale confidently.

You learn from your mistakes and use those mistakes as starting points towards change. Never embracing failure but knowing when to accept defeat. Understanding what makes you weaker but focusing on what makes you stronger.

It means that you love hard, play hard, work hard, Mommy hard, Daddy hard, wife hard, husband hard, sister hard, brother hard and friend hard!

You never skimp on challenges because you have invested your total self. This is the only way you can get over and get through things to keep it moving...the only way that you can bounce back after hitting rock bottom. This coupled with the strength, and the faith that comes from your belief and commitment to a higher power can only empower you.

And for me, it constantly means leaning on my shield of faith and understanding that God's plan for me is the only plan that will ultimately prevail. I know that over the past year it has been quite difficult for me emotionally, psychologically, and financially since the death of my beloved Dad in November, 2014.

## *How to Get Over It in 30 Days Part II*

    Over the past year, there have been many events that led me down many paths that I had never traveled before. These experiences along this road have rocked me to the core, questioned my belief system and the importance of things and people in my life but the one constant that has not changed throughout all of this has been my Faith.

    Yes, Faith has always been the shield that I lean on for hope, mercy, grace and humility. It is the spirit that moves me and allows me to know that despite and in spite of whatever may be happening, "everything will be alright."

    Through this journey, I know that I have been bent but not broken, damaged but not destroyed and tried but never convicted of failure. I am still that foot soldier emerging from the trenches and that warrior ready to do battle with devils in disguise. And now I am ready to share and teach others how to push through the pain and convicts of conscience to follow their dreams, become resilient on the road to becoming empowered.

    I will show you once again how to "Get Over It!" and "BounceBack" in spite of anything that you have gone through in your life. I know that this year has perhaps been the most difficult year of my life emotionally, psychologically and financially. I have faced challenges that should have caused me to just "give up and give in." But I couldn't so I didn't.

    I had to lean on those shields of grace, faith, and mercy just to rise out of my bed every day. Just to answer when someone called my name. Just to believe in the prayers I dutifully said each night and just to know that tomorrow was only a day away.

It was hard and in many respects it is still very hard. But what I know is that although I may not be where I want to be, but I am not where I used to be either. I know that this is because through it all I never stopped believing…I never stopped knowing that if I did *BELIEVE* then somehow, someway, it would all work out. This has been my strength and my guide, and this is what I want to teach you in this book.

I want to show you how you can still *BELIEVE* even when you feel as though you have hit rock bottom…You can still *BELIEVE* when you think that you are all alone. You can still *BELIEVE* when you question the steps God has ordered for you, and you can still *BELIEVE* when you start to wonder if God ordered any steps for you in the first place.
I leaned on the triplet shields of grace, faith, and mercy to give me the strength to believe that my life could only get better and that the path to greatness for me would be clearer.

Much of what I have written in these messages are grounded in my own growth and healing process. It comes from deep places of pain and heartache and the crevices of my soul. But you know what? It's a year later, and I am still standing, I am still smiling, and I am okay. I am walking, living, proof of the power of prayer and the strength of believing in who I am and what I do.

The inspirational messages in this book are designed to empower you to make choices that will lead you towards emotional prosperity because you deserve to be happy.

## How to Get Over It in 30 Days Part II

The *B.E.L.I.E.V.E.* system teaches you how to begin to Get Over It and steps to incorporate into your daily life. And although you may not be "fixed" in 30 days after reading this book, you will be able to think about your life in a different way.

My primary intent of this book is to provide a daily message that will inspire and empower your thought process and begin to change your behavior patterns. Remember, "although you may not be where you want to be, you don't have to be where you used to be either." Your actions make a difference.

*Dr. Adair f. White-johnson*

# Dr. Adair's B.E.L.I.E.V.E. Empowerment System

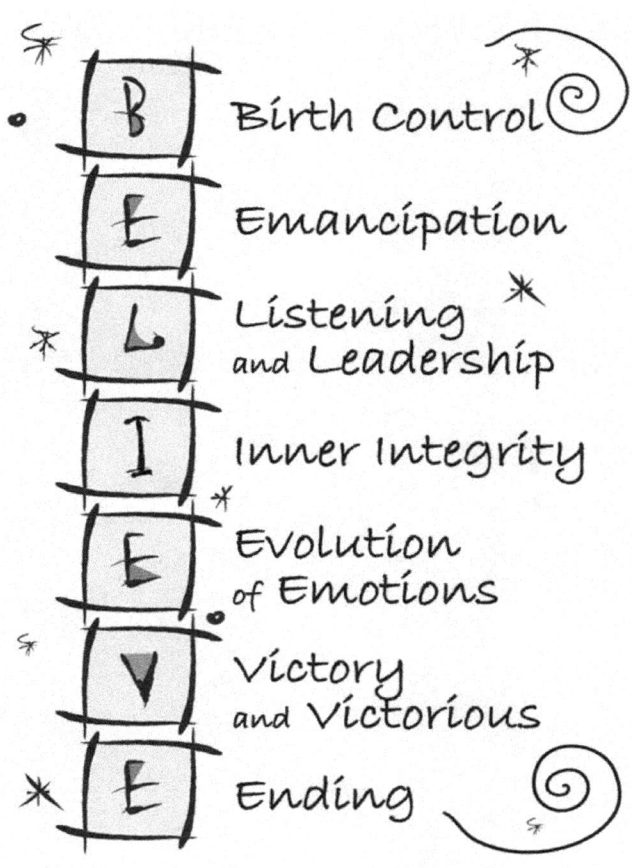

I created the **_BELIEVE_** system as a follow-up to my **_G.O. H.A.R.D_**. formula that I presented in my first books because after working with and speaking with many others I honestly think that this is a crucial missing piece of the puzzle of happiness in all of our lives. The next several pages will describe the acronym as detailed in my previous book "Get Over It! 7 Steps to Live Well with Lupus" (2014).

*Dr. Adair f. White-johnson*

## *Birth Control*

Part of knowing that you *BELIEVE* is taking your birth control for protection and filling your mind and spirit with the medication needed to sustain your faith and to anesthetize any travelling negativity that seeks to impregnate your mind by planting seeds of doubt. This is the only way to move forward with fulfilling your dreams. It is the only way to control the stones that may be thrown along the path that you take to greatness. I learned long ago to bury the negativity that existed in my life and that if I used Birth Control at the very beginning then I would be attending fewer funerals in the end.

There are times that you will need a contraceptive method to protect you from the people (i.e. family and friends) who love and know you the most. Sometimes these can be toxic relationships that your heart and spirit need protection from…If you fail to use your artillery to protect them then all of your efforts of being a foot soldier emerging from the trenches will be wasted, and you will be "sucked" into a vacuum of negativity and despair. You will believe what they tell you before you believed what is in your heart and guided by your spirit. The only way to kill the virus of negativity is to create a contraceptive method to protect you against it before it appears in your life….Your artillery.

## *Emancipation*

Bob Marley sang in his hit song "Emancipate yourself from mental slavery; none but ourselves can free our minds."

When I was a teenager, my grandmother and I lived in a small, two-bedroom apartment in Brooklyn after my mom died. There were days of happiness, and days of extreme sadness during that time. You see, while my mother was alive, I suffered physical, emotional, psychological and sexual abuse directly and indirectly under her watch. It took me many, many years to forgive her and to forgive myself, but I did. This was a critical step in freeing my mind from the mental enslavement of being a victim. I had to learn how to unlock the keys to the intellectual prison that held my rights to think for myself hostage. This has to be done in order for true emancipation to occur. We must learn to emancipate our minds, hearts and our souls from the prison wardens of negativity, hurt, and pain.

Emancipation is about letting go of all the negativity in your life…those things that are only there to hurt you and do not support you. It is learning how to truly "Let Go and Let God." Giving back to him what you just cannot handle and raise your hands in celebration. It is knowing when to walk away and to understand that just because you walk away does not mean that you have given up…It just means that you made a choice.

*Dr. Adair f. White-johnson*

## *Listening and Leadership*

**Listening**

Sometimes in our lives we are so used to being in control and organizing and setting our lives up that we fail just to sit and listen. We never hear what our hearts and bodies are telling us, and we never hear the advice that our spirit is injecting into our bloodstream, so it flows throughout our bodies. And when we do not listen, we never hear the answers to our problems.

Learning to listen to your own heart is a skill that must be learned if we plan to be happy. If we ignore the voices within, then we miss the messages that they are sending. We miss the opportunity to be true to ourselves and make a difference in our lives.

Suppose you were able to hear your heart? And hear your dreams? Would you be able to follow them more easily? Would you be able to make better choices and action plans to lead you to a positive place?

I think about instances in my life where I didn't listen to my own heart and spirit. Both of these were broken because I failed to listen....It was a hard lesson to learn but as I matured, I learned that I must listen to my needs first before I can listen to the voices of anyone else.

I really feel that we need to include exercises and activities in our daily lives that teach us how to listen to ourselves. Yes, meditation works and I feel as though prayer is the ultimate way to reach our inner beings, but sometimes reprogramming our brains to listen is one of the first steps. This can be done by just "being still" and also by writing notes to ourselves. Telling ourselves what we are thinking and feeling—having conversations with ourselves so that we truly understand our perspectives on what we are feeling. This can help us in our quest to *Get Over It* because we can create our action plans from an informed place in our minds.

I use this strategy as a part of my *BELIEVE* system because so many times we forget to hear our own voices, and this allows us to bring the volume to these silenced voices. It is a method of communicating with our inner beings so that we can make positive choices in our lives and understand our emotions. So yes, to *Get Over It* we have to recognize and understand our emotions, and we have to Listen to our hearts and mind because a double vision is needed to coherently feel.

**Leadership**

Being a Leader is not just what I do. It's a part of who I am. You see, I believe that Leadership comes from within---it comes from living in your purpose, manifesting your destiny and understanding that resiliency is the foundation of your determination.

It is the recognition that you must first "work a dream to live the dream." This requires recognizing who you are, the values you embrace, and knowing that "what's for you is what's for you." But is this easy? Of course not! But knowing essential components of resiliency is a start.

## Dr. Adair f. White-johnson

Being resilient demands that you are a chameleon of sorts --prepared to morph into life roles that require flexibility, strength, and tenacity. Searching within the crevices of your heart and soul to discover untouchable feelings, and sensations that push you to continue trying even when you think you should "give up."

It's that push, that tug that makes you feel like you can still climb that mountain with bare feet and reminds you that you can push through the pain and you can *Get Over It!* That's resiliency.

You see, knowing that you still have the fight left in you is an example of strength itself---Knowing what inspires you to dress in that warrior costume, and knowing the things that propel you towards greatness serve as the foundation of your leadership. You become that foot soldier emerging through the trenches to pull yourself up by your bootstraps so you can continue to live your life effectively. You do it because you have to. You do it because you need to. You do it because you want to. You do it because you are a Leader. And you do it because you are resilient.

Being resilient also means that you have created personal artillery to combat negativity in your life. It suggests that you have built an arsenal to protect your heart and soul from anything that seeks to threaten the positivity of your existence. Knowing that it is your weapon against self-destruction is the key defense in your struggle for significance. I think that knowing how to live your life effectively despite any odds requires that you embrace the main tenets of the "Resiliency Formula."

## How to Get Over It in 30 Days Part II

This formula includes strategies that focus on Overcoming Odds, Controlling Anger, Creating Healthy Balances, Forgiveness Techniques, Building Dreams and Reaching Destiny Points. Knowing this becomes a pivotal motivator that will allow you to conquer any trials and tribulations in your life fearlessly-- despite feelings of confusion, doubt, and disillusionment.

You see, I learned long ago that there really are six ways of knowing in life– tradition, expert opinion, logic, research, personal experience, and intuition. Although the former are excellent knowledge resources, it is the latter that my resiliency is built upon and sustained.

My intuition in my life served as the bootstrap that allowed me to pull myself up out of the pits of sadness, despair, anxiety, frustration, hopelessness and all things negative because it gave me the power to believe in my own thoughts and feelings. It is the cornerstone of my existence and the foundation of my leadership. Yes, I truly believe that we all have moments when we don't feel that we are resilient, as "strong" as we want to be, and question the true purpose of our lives.

And we already know that we are "so much" but we are striving to be "so much more" but we are unsure how to get there. We know that dreams don't come with a warranty or guarantee, but we know that being resilient is at the core of our dreams, and allows us to remain effective leaders.

## Dr. Adair f. White-johnson

In my life, I've used my leadership skills to make a positive difference in the lives of others as well…The key is an effective leader of my own life first. Knowing what serves as the nourishment for my resiliency is mandatory, and I know that the shield it leans on is Faith. I know that my Faith is stronger than my pain so I know that it can withstand the weight of my resiliency.

## *Inner Integrity*

Inner Integrity can be defined as "the quality of being honest and having strong moral principles; moral uprightness." I think that sometimes in our lives we lose a bit of integrity to ourselves, and we begin to lie to ourselves, so we are able to live in the reality that we have created. The problem is that when we start to believe those lies we start to lose ourselves in a world that we created. Denying who we are, so we do not have to deal with everything that comes with being ourselves.

Sometimes I am guilty of living in denial when I am wearing my "superwoman" cape, and there are many tasks that must be completed. I convince myself that I am the only one who can complete the job effectively and that I can do it all by myself.

I lie to myself when I want to help others at the expense of taking care of myself. I am untrue to my own feelings in an effort to "do right" by others. I know. I get it. I know I am guilty of trying to be all things to all people, and I ended up being nothing to myself when I lacked my inner integrity.

When you lack integrity then what moral principles do you have to lead and guide your dreams? Your goals? Your possibilities? How do you know that you are on the right path to happiness?

You cannot live in a vacuum of ignorance and think that life will be okay...Many folks live with this mindset because they believe that it is easier. For some it appears to be a simple existence --- to live in a "comfortable Hell" than to strive to live in an "uncomfortable Heaven."

So we all begin to lie to ourselves, becoming like dogs chasing our tails….running around in circles and not making any progress.

You need Inner Integrity to move forward and make a difference in your life. Inner Integrity is a necessary and essential part of my *BELIEVE* system because if you cannot live in your own truth then, you will find yourself living in another world of lies. Doing this will compromise your emotional state and will prohibit you from emotionally evolving. You will become stagnated, and will be unable to make any progress in moving towards change.

*How to Get Over It in 30 Days Part II*

## *Evolution of Emotions*

Knowing and accepting that your emotions change over time is a step towards making positive changes in your life. Recognizing that what you may have wanted last year is different than what you want and need this year is perfectly fine. Just because you ate popcorn at the movie theater last time does not mean that you want it again this time…It is okay to change how you feel, and not feel guilty because of it.

Our emotions grow and change, and that's okay because we do as well. Some of us never thought we could forgive someone that did something wrong to us, so we hold on to that anger and frustration because we think that it would be wrong if we forgave the perpetrator. We hold on because it is easier than to forgive. But know that just because we forgive someone does not mean that we have to allow them back into our lives. It simply means that we forgave them. That is what happens when your emotions evolve…It puts us in uncomfortable positions, and it challenges the essence of who we really are. But we need to do this in order to change. We must first change the way we think before we can change the way we behave.

*Dr. Adair f. White-johnson*

## *Victory and Victorious*

Joel Osteen once said that you should proclaim "I am a Victor and not a Victim so I can be Victorious!"

Oh, how right he is….he teaches about being a palm tree….that when the hurricanes come blowing in your direction you bend, but you are not broken because you are able to bounce back. You are not like oak trees where you snap, break and come crashing down…You are built to bend, and that's why you are able to handle so much on in your life.

Please understand this, and embrace that when the next storm blows in your direction you will waste valuable time focusing on the fear of being broken and being a victim, instead of creating action plans to become victorious. Know that you are built to bend and that at the end of the day everything will be alright.

Don't let your fear paralyze your Faith so that you don't want to take chances because you are afraid you will be broken…Know that you can be damaged, but you are never destroyed…This is what Victory is all about, and it should shape your everyday philosophy. You have to believe that you can live victoriously, and that although life can be tough and sometimes challenging to deal with, you can be confident that you can weather any storm ---You will still be standing after any hurricane winds have blown in your direction.

## How to Get Over It in 30 Days Part II

      I believe that if you continuously lean on the quadruple shields of grace, faith, mercy and humility, you will know that you will ultimately be victorious in any situation. It is all dependent upon your mindset and your approach to the situation. You see, I choose to take control of those things in my life that I can, and for those that I cannot, I choose to believe that I still have a voice.

      I cannot allow myself to be mentally enslaved to negativity or become a provocative victim where I entice hardship and struggle to come my way. Instead, I serve as my own advocate, build my artillery, and lean on those shields that I've been describing in this book. Once I am assured that these things are in place then I already know, at the end of the challenge, I will be victorious because is it a mindset, an attitude and an approach and I have the *Victor* mentality to ensure that everything will be alright because I am exactly where I am supposed to be in this life. You can do this too…you just have to trust and believe.

*Dr. Adair f. White-johnson*

# *E*nding

Creating life lesson plans that help shape our lives helps us to realize what we need to do in order get what we want. We also learn that if things do not fit the scheme we have created, we must end it. I like to compare it to a teacher creating lesson plans for the students. Typically there are specific behavioral objectives/goals presented and then the teacher designs activities to reach those goals. The teacher attempts to adhere to the activities because all of them serve a purpose, and the teacher knows that if it does not serve a purpose, then they do not need it. Hmmmm…

What if we applied this same philosophy to things and people in our lives? What if we created strategies and activities that were specifically aligned with our goals? What if we diminished those factors that prohibited us from reaching our dreams? Supposed we learned how to live with Lupus so that we could achieve our dreams?

Hmmmm….To accomplish this, you have to learn how to release those things that do not serve a purpose. You have to learn how to *END* the relationships and situations that are not aligned with your dreams. Using the main tenets of my *BELIEVE* system helps you to determine what needs to be ended in your life so you can achieve your happiness despite of whatever you have been through in your life.

*How to Get Over It in 30 Days Part II*

Learning how to end the things that cause you pain.
Learning how to end the things that are not good for you.
Learning how to figure out what is good for you.
Learning how to determine what you don't need and what doesn't work for you.
Learning how to end the toxic relationships in your life.
Learning how to end the toxic feelings you have inside of you.
Learning how to end things that you should have never started.
Learning how to BEGIN with the END in mind.

This is just the beginning of the transformation of your thought process. It is life transforming, and it requires a paradigm shift about the way you have been approaching your life. It requires you to take a look at the life that you are leading and how you are leading it….It demands that you no longer put Band-Aids on gunshot wounds and instead, learn how to do the surgery so you can live an enriched and fulfilled life despite your past heartache and pain. Following the seven steps of the *BELIEVE* system can help you accomplish this.

I also hope that you find strength in the words that I share with you in this book, and they help lead you to your destiny of happiness. I know you can get there, and I know you can do this because you are a warrior and a survivor. You have to tools you need to live in your purpose and to embrace your gifts….I believe in you and I know that you can *Get Over It*! You just have to **BELIEVE.**

## Dr. Adair f. White-johnson

Now that you understand the foundation of this book you are ready to begin your 30-day journey to "Get Over It!" I would encourage you to read one message a day so that you can really understand the lesson and apply it to your daily life. You will also discover that the book has quite a few "extra" messages…That's my gift to you…I just couldn't stop writing, and I just couldn't stop sharing. Enjoy. Be motivated. Be inspired. Be empowered.

*How to Get Over It in 30 Days Part II*

# DAY 1
## *"Football Anyone?"*

Sometimes we are exactly where we are supposed to be but we just don't know it yet.

On Saturday, I went to my son's football game and was reminded of more than what a dynamic player he is. You see as I watched the game I was able to see once again how God works in his own way....
During one of the plays, the coaches noticed that they were short one player on the field. In an effort to not receive a penalty they yelled at the closest player to them, #4, to "Get out on the field!" He ran out on the field without any instructions about where to go and what to do. He was clearly confused but somehow got into position. You could tell from his 12-year-old body language that he was a bit unsure and lacked confidence at that moment but nonetheless he was there and "almost" ready.

When the whistle blew, and the play began the opposing quarterback decided to throw/pass the ball to one of his players. At this precise moment, #4 jumped up and between two other players and caught the ball. An interception. He then ran the ball 30 yards for a touchdown. Wow.

You see, sometimes we are exactly where we are supposed to be, but we just don't know it. We are exactly where God has placed us and where he wants us. Like player #4 we may be a bit nervous and a little confused but we need to remember to lean on those shields of Grace, Faith, Mercy and Humility for the strength we need. There will be times in our lives when we are just "thrown in" without warning and without instructions. But we cannot give in and give up...

Sometimes we will just have to trust and believe and know that everything will be alright. We know this because we know that God orders our steps and we are on the path that he has created for us.

Sometimes this may be the road less traveled and other times it may be the uphill trail from the depths of the valley. But we know we are here because we are supposed to be.

We are not "special" because we are going through "stuff" in our lives. We are not "special" because we are hurting.
We are not "special" because we are scared. Confused. Hurt.
And we are not "special" because we don't have a clear understanding of our purpose in life.

We are at this point in our lives because this is what God has created for us.
And sometimes we may go in the wrong direction but he always equips us with the right type of compass so we can find our way back.

## How to Get Over It in 30 Days Part II

And when we feel as though we are just "thrown in" we have to remember that we have Faith so we can jump up like #4 to catch whatever is thrown our way.

Our Faith will supply us with hope, strength, tenacity, diligence and dedication that we need to help us push through pain and confusion. It will force us to make the right "plays" like #4 in this game called "life."

Stop questioning your purpose in life.
Stop believing that God is "picking on you" and not "there for you."
It's simply not true.
You are where you are because that is where you are supposed to be.

And your "touchdown" is coming but you must first trust and believe when God sends you out on the field even when you are just "almost ready." Just like #4.

I often tell others "I am not where I want to be, but I am not where I used to be either." And I'm okay with that because I know wherever I am, my God is right by my side, so I know my "touchdown" is coming soon...

So, let's play ball!

## DAY 2
### *"Grace"*

I am awakening today feeling grateful.

While I already know that this has perhaps been one of the most challenging times in my life, I also know that I have not gone through all of this for anything.

In a special way I feel chosen because I don't think that God assigns us more than we can handle and if he gave all of these hardships to me this year then he believes in my tenacity to handle it.

Many times I have felt bent, but I knew I was not broken.
I have felt damaged, but I knew I was not destroyed. I have found triumph in tragedy.
And the strength in strife.

You see there have been many nights where I have cried myself to sleep asking the question "why?" or "why me?"
And then the very next morning I wake up just relieved to be still breathing and all I can say is "Thank You God."

Sometimes we just go through stuff to become better.
To become stronger.
To become more faithful.
To become more grounded.
And to become more resilient.

## *How to Get Over It in 30 Days Part II*

Sometimes we may need our lives actually to change to know really that we really needed a change to begin with.
In many ways, my emotional, psychological, social and financial well beings have been challenged this year.

And I think I conquered the challenge because I'm Still Standing, and I feel like a foot soldier emerging from the trenches to become a Warrior...

And although I'm still figuring it all out I am so grateful that I have the mind to search for answers, the spirit to believe I will find the answers, the humility to admit I need answers and the obedience to accept the answers.

So yes, this has been a rough year for me but in my many ways it has also been the best because I learned the greatest lesson of all...

God is still in control and whatever I've been through in my life is nothing compared to trying to live a life without God's Faith in me...

**Lesson:** Life may feel painful right now and you are struggling to figure it all out but know that everything is going to be alright in God's time... Just keep leaning on those shields of Grace, Faith and Mercy and you'll know everything will be alright!

# DAY 3
## *"I Have to Let YOU Go!!"*

You can't steal my joy because you didn't put it there.
And you can't ask me to return my happiness because
I didn't get it from you.

You see, my purpose is not defined by your existence
and my emotional sobriety is not dependent upon
your approval.

I am independent, free-spirited, priceless, and honest.
And you can't hold me back.

My dreams are bigger than your negative reality.
And my faith is stronger than your spiteful words.

My spirit is full of inspiration
And my soul has already been committed to
excellence.

So you can't touch this.

I already know that I am "so much" but I've also
learned that I can be "so much" more.

With or without your support.

The key is to hold on to my own positive energy, to
never limit my possibilities, to never allow my
disabilities to disable my abilities and to keep on
dreaming.

## How to Get Over It in 30 Days Part II

See I know that when I finish one dream I've got to start working on the next one.

And when I'm walking on a lonely road that may be less traveled then it is actually okay.

Because God is actually right by my side.
And he supports me.

So my friend, if you can't be there for me, with me and next to me then you can't be beside me.

My life is too precious to waste on your negativity, and I won't allow you to steal things that you never gave to me in the first place...

>My hopes.
>My dreams.
>My faith.
>My spirit.
>My heart.
>My soul.
>My gifts.
>My talents.
>My determination.
>My happiness.
>My ..

You can't have them because they just don't belong to you.

*I am. I can. I will. I do.*

And it's because of who I am and not because of you.

## Dr. Adair f. White-johnson

Thanks be to God.

***Lesson:*** If "they" cannot support you then what purpose do they serve in your life? If they have no purpose then, they should have no space...It's time to "Let go" of some people in your life who only bring negative energy and strife...Let them Go.

*How to Get Over It in 30 Days Part II*

# DAY 4
# *"I'm a THIEF."*

Sometimes the only thief in our lives is ourselves.

We steal our own joy by poisoning it with negative thoughts.
We steal our own happiness by denying our dreams the opportunity to flourish.
We steal our ability to love others unconditionally by smothering it with past heartache and pain.
And we steal our own faith by not trusting and believing that God orders our steps and has already created our master plans.

I've robbed myself many times in my life when I just didn't trust my instincts.
So I never followed through on some ideas.

Hmmmm...One of those thoughts could have been "the one" that made all of my dreams come true.
But I stole it from myself by never allowing myself to receive it, plan it and then put it into action.

I stole many precious moments in my relationships with my family and friends by not allowing them "in" to help me when I hurt badly and really needed them...

When I needed encouragement and inspiration to get over something.

## Dr. Adair f. White-johnson

When I was intent on being "Superwoman" during the time when I needed "SuperLove..."

So I stole emotional bonding with people who love me and wanted to "be there" for me...

And I robbed myself of the chance to stop being an enabler and taking the responsibility of the actions of others when I was, unfortunately, violated by a man I trusted and then I blamed myself.
I made excuses for him, and I questioned my own actions and focused on what I could have done differently.
But I never told my story until decades later when it felt "safe" and I truly understood that it wasn't my fault.

So I robbed myself of living a life knowing that there are some things in life that happen to you that just aren't your fault but you still have to learn and heal from them so you can move forward.

And, you don't have to make excuses for people who hurt you.
I was a thief who stole opportunities to learn more.
To do more.
To be more.
To live more.
I thought I knew it all so I didn't and wouldn't listen to the advice of others, so I stole the power of knowledge from myself.

## How to Get Over It in 30 Days Part II

I crept into my own head on many nights, stole my confidence and convinced myself that the time wasn't right for me to try new things, explore other options or dare to dream.
Because of this I limited my possibilities, confused my purpose and challenged my destiny.

Sometimes with a negative attitude I've even tried to steal the smiles off the faces of unsuspecting individuals through my callous actions and by injecting the sarcasm into my words.
By doing this, I stole the gift of treating others the way I want/should be treated.

I've stolen memories from myself because I just didn't want to think about "stuff" anymore. But when I did this I also erased many good thoughts and amazing experiences that were highlights of my life...

Just because I was afraid of some of those memories and how they made me feel...

And because I sometimes have the insatiable appetite to control the world around me so I can be "happy," I steal the chance to hear the thoughts of others, to experience creative differences, celebrate individual concepts and embrace dynamic ideas.

So yes, I admit it...I am a thief.
I've stolen too much from myself throughout my lifetime.
I'm guilty.
But now I'm ready to turn myself in.
Ready to "do my time."

I'm okay with being tried and convicted so that I can be sentenced to a lifetime of happiness.

You see all those things that I stole?
I don't need them in my life...Those things are toxins that only serve the purpose of poisoning my heart, mind, body and soul...

I'd rather be in a prison locked away with the things that will empower and motivate me...
Lock me away with my spirit of positivity and my faith in God.
Being able to lean on my shields of grace, faith, and mercy...

Yes...I'll take the lifetime sentence like this.
I deserve it because this punishment really does fit the crime.
I need it so I can know better to do better.
And I'm guilty as charged.
I'm a *THIEF*.

***Lesson:*** Sometimes we accuse the wrong people of stealing from us but if we look into the mirror we may find the biggest thief of them all. Are you a thief??? Are you guilty as charged?

## DAY 5
## *"Prayers Don't Stop!"*

Sometimes we only ask Jesus to take the wheel and steer our lives when we feel things are crumbling around us.

Sometimes we pray much harder when we feel as though we no longer have control over things that are happening in our lives.

Sometimes we find ourselves on our knees praying, wanting, wishing and hoping much harder when things are not going "well."

But I think, and I know that we need to ask for God's blessings, praying for God's will, and hoping for God's direction when things are going magnificent in our lives as well.

You see for me that is the time when it feels like everything is going "right" and I can see success all around me. I already understand that because to "whom much is given, much is required."

Sometimes I also get scared because I know that God has placed before me things that can and will be done, but I must first rise to the challenge...It is at this time that I think I need to "feel" him more in my spirit and in my soul so my prayers are deeper and more frequent.

## Dr. Adair f. White-johnson

So it is during these times of success with my life is going well when I don't see perils of danger right in front of me, when my hopes and my dreams appear to come true that I am on my knees praying to God lead me and guide me.

It is now that I am leaning on my shields of grace faith and mercy.
And of course, humility.

It is when I am at my *BEST* that I need him the most.
It is now that I must use my faith to walk alongside my doubts and fear.
And use my humility to strengthen my back as I lean over to pull others up to prosperity.

Yes, it is during these times when my dreams have come true, when I feel the strongest, the happiest and the wealthiest that I must pray the most because the responsibility is the greatest.

Yes, even I times of immense happiness, prayer still changes everything.

***Lesson:*** Prayers do not stop after blessings are received.

# DAY 6
## *"One Drop at a Time…"*

Sometimes changing the way you think is just so damn hard.
Your heart wants to, but your mind plays tricks on you and makes you believe that you can't.

When you want to be "out" of love with someone because it's "just time" and you feel like you love them longer and harder you feel so weak.

And when you want to change that job because it just doesn't meet your needs anymore you feel so scared of what the future may bring.

And changing the way you think about certain situations so you can maintain relationships and "peace" in your life seems like a daunting task.

So you second guess yourself.

You want to do the right thing, so you pray for guidance.
You want to feel the right thing, so you pray for inspiration.
But yet, it is just so damn hard.

See changing the way we think requires a shift in our ideological, philosophical, spiritual and emotional paradigms.

## Dr. Adair f. White-johnson

Ideological, philosophical, spiritual and emotional paralysis can have the worst impact than physical paralysis.

If you don't feel anything in your heart and your soul and you don't use your brain then you have paralyzed your ability to live a happy life...you can live a fulfilled life with a physical paralysis but I'm not convinced that you can do it if you are living with a spiritual paralysis.

It demands that we acknowledge our greatest strengths may also be our greatest weaknesses.
And it requires our resiliency in the raw.
We have to reject failure as an option.
And embrace success as the only solution.

We need to want the mindset change so badly that we are willing to change our lifestyle and our "life-beings" because of it.
We have to remove the layers of fear, anguish, despair, doubt, shame and "fakeness" to begin to change our minds to live healthier lifestyles.

This is all the stuff our change gets caught up in.

Remember that just like that bucket of water that can be eventually filled with one drop at a time, your mindset can shift with one thought at a time...
Healthy minds lead to healthy behavior which takes us down the path to a healthy life.

Is it hard? Uhhh, YEAH!

## *How to Get Over It in 30 Days Part II*

It is easier to live in that comfortable hell than to strive for existence in an uncomfortable heaven, so we settle to remain in the mindset that we've always had.

We are so afraid…we have that fear of the unknown and that "drama-free" zone that we don't allow ourselves to grow and become what we are destined to be.

But dreams don't come with a warranty or guarantee so we need to change our thought process to achieve them.

There is no "master" plan to change our minds ….We simply begin by recognizing that the change has to begin from within…

But the change can hurt so bad that we just don't want to do it even though we already know that we own the power of change so we must exercise that power and begin with ourselves…

If you change the way you think, you will change the way you behave….If you change the way you behave, then you will change the way you live….

And I know it takes courage…but I also know that we are all born with courage but it's when we use it at the right time that makes us courageous.

Changing our minds is the first step in that process….

*Dr. Adair f. White-johnson*

***Lesson:*** Just like you can fill a bucket one drop at a time you can make changes one move at a time...

*How to Get Over It in 30 Days Part II*

# DAY 7
# *"Just Do It!"*

I am often asked "How do you do it?" and "Where do you get the strength from?

I don't always have a clear answer because I can't always explain it myself.

But what I do know is that I lean on the shields of Grace, Faith, Mercy and Humility every day and that provides me with the strength that I need to Get Over It, Get Through It and Keep It Moving.

You see failure for me really is not an option, nor has it ever been.
Giving up is not on my agenda either.
I will choose to "walk away" from a situation or person but to "give up" is just not a plan for me...

And I can't always explain what I do, why I do it and how I can dig into the depths of my soul and imagination to find a way to do it.

All I know is that a voice is screaming inside of me to "Just do it! Just do it! Just do it!"

So I figure out a way to just get it done
.
And some of my plans, strategies and techniques don't always work but it's kind of like my dreams, when I'm finished with one I just find and start another that will work.

I just keep trying until I get it right.
But leaning on those shields is what really propels me forward.

Every day I am reminded me that I don't walk on this path alone -- that God has ordered my steps, and I'm only traveling along the road that he has paved for me.

So I know that I am never doing it alone.

And I have many supporters but there are also many haters out there as well who do not wish the best for me and do not support the dreams that I have. And there are some who blame me for ANY troubles that may come my way.

But you see I don't answer to them.
I don't have to live their dreams.
I don't have to walk in their shadows.
I don't have to fear them because they are not the boss of me.

God is.

My God is the only one who leads me and guides me every day.
And so whatever success I may have achieved in my life I first give thanks to him--my God.

## How to Get Over It in 30 Days Part II

And I continue to get out there to grind and hustle because I firmly believe that nobody ever gave me anything but a chance and I took that chance and made it into great opportunities that have led to my successes.
I work hard for the things that I have and the experiences in my life.
I know that I own my dreams, and they are my responsibility to make them come true.
I also know that dreams do not come with a warranty or guarantee, and I have to work a dream to live the dream.

Now if this is what makes the difference between the person on my left and the person on my right and myself then maybe that explains why I have been able to accomplish what I have in my life but I am not going to apologize for it.

I'm going to stand strong because of it.

Yes, I embrace everything in my life.
The good, the bad and the ugly.

And I have faith in knowing "everything is because it is what is."
And "what is for me is for me."
I take it all, and I use it as lessons learned.
For me, lessons learned are indeed blessings earned.

I am.<br>
I can.<br>
I will.<br>
I do.

## Dr. Adair f. White-johnson

And it is all because of the steps that God has ordered for me.

> I follow my plan.
> I work that plan.
> I hustle that plan.

When I decided to walk away from a six-figure income a year some people thought I was crazy but I knew in my heart it was time to follow my next dream and sometimes you have to make those difficult choices in order to be happy.

Yes, I am happy despite and in spite of it all the good, the bad and ugly every morning when I wake up I'm thankful.
I'm blessed.
I'm faithful, and I continue to lean on my shields of Grace, Mercy, Faith and Humility.

Sometimes in my life it has been rough but other times it has been totally awesome but either way <u>it is</u> my life and I have to live it in the best way I know how.

So what I'm saying to you is know who you are.
Live in your purpose.
Push through the pain.
And have faith knowing that God is on your side.

That's really my story.
It's really the center of who I am, what I do and how I do it...And I'm sticking to it.

*How to Get Over It in 30 Days Part II*

***Lesson:*** Just know how to be you. Just know what works for you. And just believe.

# DAY 8
## *"The Bottom Line"*

The bottom line is that you are responsible for your own dreams…

You cannot expect anyone else to make your dreams a reality for you.

You have to create your dream and work your dream to live your dream…That's your responsibility so don't expect others to do it for you.

The one thing that I have learned throughout my life experience is that the more you depend on others will be the more that you will learn to depend on yourself because folks just won't get it done for you.

But why should they? Is it their dream? Is it their investment? Folks can support you to infinity and beyond with their love and positive thoughts but don't wait for <u>anyone</u> to do things for you…

They mean well, but they have their own dreams to fulfill so you can't expect them to work on yours. Sad, but it is ultimately true.

You are the only one who can make your dreams become a reality for you so begin to create your plan of action.

## How to Get Over It in 30 Days Part II

When developing your path to your destiny you should include those things that are "perfect" so you can always see what you are trying to achieve but also include the "worst possible scenario" so that you are well aware of what could go wrong.

Know that the path you take could be the road less traveled but that's okay because that only means that there is more room for you to navigate on the road to greatness.

Know that your path may be full of pebbles and rocks but those are only the stepping stones you have to climb to achieve your dream.

And know that it may not be "easy" but it is "easiest" if you remain positive and grounded.

There may hear a lot of words such as be "No, Maybe, and I'll See" before you finally hear that "Yes" but that's just a part of the movement…

Be prepared for the work…get your mind right and know that this is what you really want to do because at the end of the day it is your dream that you are following, and you are responsible for it.

Some folks may interpret your confidence as self-arrogance and others will view you as a "pillar of strength" as you struggle for your significance in your dream.

### Dr. Adair f. White-johnson

Be prepared for that as well but know that you are on a mission to work that dream to live that dream...despite and in spite of others.
It's okay to question yourself, check yourself and change yourself along the way but never lose sight of who you really are...

You may have to "play some games" to get where you want/need to be but know that these are just games you are playing and remember who you really are under it all...

So, I've said this before but it is appropriate again...

*What happens to a dream deferred?*

Nothing. Absolutely nothing.
Don't let it happen.
Period.

Your dreams are your responsibility...they don't belong to anyone else so don't give them away...

Nurture and nurse those dreams as though you gave physical birth to them...
Treat them as though they are your children...
Most folks do not give their children up for adoption so don't give your dreams away either.
Love them.
Respect them and work for them so that they ultimately remain positive dreams and not scary nightmares...

*How to Get Over It in 30 Days Part II*

Ah yes, those dreams are real, and the responsibility is really yours…
Take the responsibility and make it a reality.

***Lesson:*** The Dream is Real. Work it to Live it.

*Dr. Adair f. White-johnson*

# DAY 9
## *"The Masks I Wear"*

Just because you can't see my pain doesn't mean it's not there.
Just because you don't see my tears doesn't mean I'm not wailing inside.

And just because I don't tell you everything doesn't mean I haven't shared something.

You see, I hurt every day and my soul cries all the time but I also trust and believe.
I know that tomorrow is only a day away.
I know that you can't always take my pain away.
Because you didn't put it there.

And I know that my steps have been already ordered.
So I smile every day.
And I am thankful for my moments of peace.
And become that foot soldier emerging through the trenches...

Fighting battles of the unknown and standing as that warrior of strength.

> It's just what I do.
> It's just who I am.
> It's just how I live.

*How to Get Over It in 30 Days Part II*

My faith is stronger than my pain.
And my hope is higher than my hurt.
And I just believe.

But remember, you can always ask me "How are you today?" and that reminds me that you still care.

***Lesson:*** You never know what others are going through. We all wear masks every day to shield our heartache and pain. Sometimes we just have to care just a little more to find out more, to help more and to be more...

# DAY 10
## *"Gardening Tools"*

Toxic people in your life are like weeds growing in the grass....

Some of them look as green as grass but will still kill the garden.

Others are big and stand tall, but we spend a lot of time trying to dismantle all the little ones around it because we often miss the larger weeds since they may "blend in."

But toxic people, like weeds, will continue to grow and destroy anything healthy around it.

Healthy relationships.
Healthy minds.
Healthy spirits.
Healthy dreams.

They will strip the heart of the positive nourishment needed to produce stronger lives and achieve personal goals.

Toxic people simply destroy.
Just like the weeds...

Strangling opportunities for success.
Smothering air passages used for breaths of revitalized spirits and rejuvenated hopes.

## How to Get Over It in 30 Days Part II

If they are not removed, they will continue to grow stronger and threaten the viability of our existence...just like the weeds.

So begin to search through your garden of friends to determine if you have dangerous weeds living among the healthiest of grass...

If not, your "garden" will be killed.

***Lesson:*** Gather your gardener tools and "get to diggin'!"

# DAY 11
## "My Faith is Stronger than my Pain."

Heartache is like no other pain we have experienced. It drains our energy, drains our spirits, and we are exhausted through the pain.

We cannot see it.
We cannot touch it.
We cannot smell it.
We cannot hear it.

But we can FEEL it, and we know that it's there.
And it hurts so bad.

But we cannot see or touch God in our lives either but we know he is there...

We know that by living in our purpose, leaning on our shields of grace, faith, mercy and humility that we will be healed.
We know through the power of God's Love and Faith we will find the strength to begin our healing process....

And begin to feel whole again.
You see, although heartache is real, the presence of Faith in our lives is a reality as well.

## How to Get Over It in 30 Days Part II

Faith trumps pain.
Faith heals pain.
Faith allows you to push through the pain and ultimately release it.

*Your Faith is stronger than your pain.*

So although we know heartache is real and we feel it throughout our mind, bodies and souls, we should remember that it is the presence of Faith that will allow us to "Get Over It, Get through It and Keep it Moving..."

***Lesson:*** If Faith the size of a mustard seed can move mountains then it can certainly heal your pain. Trust and believe.

*Dr. Adair f. White-johnson*

# DAY 12
## *"I Will Survive!"*

I remember many years ago singing and dancing to the song "I will Survive!"

If was sort of an anthem for many and I knew that the words spoke to me and my life situation at the time.

You see, even as a young girl I had figured out what I needed to "survive."

And it didn't come in the form of a big house, expensive car, and designer clothes.

What I needed was substance for my soul ---nutrients of resiliency.

I needed to know that although I would never walk on water, I could float on the wings of the Guardian Angels who would take care of me.

And although I couldn't part the waters myself to make a passage, I could walk along the path that was already created for me and take the steps that had been ordered for my life a long time ago.

I knew that I needed a belief system that required me to trust and believe in things I couldn't see, words I couldn't hear and stuff I couldn't touch.

## *How to Get Over It in 30 Days Part II*

I knew that on the other side of each mountain I had to climb that there was joy in the valley below...I just needed to get there.
My survival skills meant that each time I fell down, the stronger I was when I got up because I would rise with more knowledge gained.

No regrets. Only lessons learned.

I learned to survive using my tears to release and wash away misguided anger, doubt, misery, and confusion.

And I knew I would survive.

I had to become that foot soldier emerging through the trenches to recognize and understand that the battle was not mine alone.

But I didn't have to walk through the "shadow of death" to "fear no evil" because I knew that my God had cloaked my life with the essential tools to become prosperous.

And, he had armed me with my shields of grace, mercy, faith and humility to lean on when evil came my way.

Surviving for me was more than simply "living" and "existing."
It meant learning to love me.

Learning to become self-sufficient.
Learning to trust my own decisions.
Learning to live in my purpose.
Learning to know myself and what I wanted truly.
Learning to follow my dreams...and when one dream ended, find another one.
Learning to believe in the things I was capable of doing and not berating myself about the things I could not.
Learning that I just can't be all things to all people all the time and still be "me" to myself.
Learning to appreciate "tomorrow is only a day away" so despite what I'm going through today, the sun will rise again in a few hours.
Learning that I must be a woman of my word because others depend on what I say to them.
Learning that it's okay to be "independent, free-spirited, priceless and honest.
Learning just to allow myself to learn all of these things.

You see, learning how to survive is a part of our struggle for significance...

It's a part of our natural born resiliency and our inherent need to be happy.
We need it.
We want it.
And we gotta have it.
So go get it!

***Lesson:*** Know what's in your "survival kit" so you know how to survive --- to live happy and healthy and to "Get Over It!"

# DAY 13
## *"More"*

Some days I wake up, and I just want to be so much more…

I want to dream more, love more and feel more.
I want to give more, accept more and do more.
I want to dig into my soul more.
I want to pray more.
I want to be successful more.
I want to be independent more.
I want to be rich more.
I want to learn more.
I want to be confident more.
I want to be courageous more.
I want to be healthy more.
I want to be happy more.
I want to be funny more.
I want to smile more and laugh more.
I even want to be cute more.
And I want to believe in me more.
But most of all I want to be thankful and faithful more.

I deserve all of this….And More.

**Lesson:** There is always "more" but sometimes you are already the "most" because God created you just as you are. Begin to ask yourself "why" you need "more" of anything…That may tell you what you have "less" of...

*Dr. Adair f. White-johnson*

# DAY 14
## *"My Faith Moves My Mountains"*

It's funny how just when we think we are "over" something or someone it only takes one instance to remind us that we are not.

When your heart is broken there is not a surgery that can piece it back together to it's original form.
There will always be the stitches to show how it was repaired and then the scar to remind you of the wound.
And the time it takes to heal is never known because each hurt is so different and the depth and breadth of the hurt changes with each situation.

It's scary to think that you are "over it" and then you realize that it still hurts.

So what can you do?

Hmmmm...Probably not much at all.

Buttttt....We can always try.

We don't always own the power of love and pain.
We can't help who we love, and we can only limit our pain, but we are going to feel.
That's what makes us uniquely human.
And we when we sometimes feel, that brings us pain.

## *How to Get Over It in 30 Days Part II*

But we can lean on our shields of faith and know that tomorrow is just a day away.
That after the rain, the sun eventually comes out.
That after the winter, Spring always comes.
That after the complex twists and turns in the road, there will be a straight-away coming up, that after dipping deep in the valley of despair we will start climbing up the hills and mountains to reach our happy places.

That after the labor pains, there is a birth that will remind us of the wonder of life.
That after teaching, there is a lesson learned.

That after hard work, there is always time to play and that after we have drained our minds/bodies of self-made positivity then our faith is there to replenish us.

So you see, although there are some things that we may NEVER get over in our lives we can still get through them.

While we can't necessarily control who we love or when we hurt, we can control the effect it can have on our lives.

Having faith helps us to know that the hurt will soon be filled with the happy and the pain will be swapped out for pleasure. Faith does that for you.

Yes, hurt hurts. And we want it to go away.

I absolutely hate it when it comes back...that "surprise bumping into" meeting, the old photo that you come across, a song you hear and simple birthday that you remember can stir those emotions that cause you to hurt. You just never know what will trigger these feelings... But what you can hold on to is that your faith will pull you through it all.

I've said this many times and I'm going to say it again here....Faith is a miraculous healer... It's a "mover" and a "shaker."

If faith the size of a mustard seed can move mountains then, it can surely move you...

Know it, Have it, Empower yourself, Embrace yourself in it and Love yourself for believing in it.

***Lesson:*** You can't always control your pain, but you can always have faith that you will get through it.

# DAY 15
## *"Don't Worry About a Thing..."*

Sometimes I wonder how strong my back is...

I think about the weight it carries and the burdens it bears...
I think about how often it has been bent over but has never been actually broken.
And how it had to stand erect when difficult situations demanded its attention.

Sometimes I wonder how tough my heart really is...
I think about how many times it has been broken but yet I've been able to put all the pieces back together again.
I think about often it has been misused and abused.
And how it may have been damaged but never destroyed.

Sometimes I wonder how deep my soul is...
I think about how far down inside of my core I've had to reach in some situations to understand it...
To know it.
To fix it.
To *"Get Over It."*

Although I spend time thinking about my back, my heart, and my soul, I never question my faith....
I know that it is what allows my back to remain strong, my heart open and my soul free...

## Dr. Adair f. White-johnson

It is what motivates me.
Inspires me.
Empowers me.
And gives me the strength to push through the pain, to recognize that tomorrow is only a day away and that for each mountain I climb, it puts me closer to heaven.

With my life comes the highs and the lows but in between it all my faith sustains me.
And allows me to remember that despite and in spite of it all, God is on my side.

And "every lil' thing is gonna be alright."

***Lesson:*** "Don't worry about a thing cuz every lil' thing is gonna be alright..." (Bob Marley)

*How to Get Over It in 30 Days Part II*

# DAY 16
# *"Don't SAVE it, USE it!"*

I know we've all heard folks say "I'm saving the best for last."

Hmmmm...

If they do that then what are they giving me right now?
Raise your hand if you want folks to give you their "half-ass" best at any time.

Didn't think so.

So why do we do it to ourselves?

Why do we give our best to others and try to "save the best for last" for ourselves?

The problem is that by the time we get to ourselves there is usually nothing left or just a little bit leftover.

And then we wonder why we are dissatisfied and can't reach our goals in love, happiness, and success.

You see, you need to remember that you are "the best" and so you only deserve "the best."

Not just from others but from yourself first.

You've got gifts. Share them with yourself first.
You've got talents. Cultivate them with yourself first.
You've got skills. Train them for yourself first.
You've got faith. Believe in it for yourself first.
You've got God. Listen to him for yourself first.

Yes, it's okay to "do you" first...to give yourself wholly and freely to you first in order to be happy...That's how it's supposed to be.

If you can't please yourself first then how will you know how to please others?
If you can't give yourself the "best" then how do you really know what your "best" looks like to give to others?

Hmmmm...

"Save the best for last" just doesn't work when you are trying to put your best foot forward first. You will end up in the "last place" in line for success if you keep giving away all of your "good stuff" to everyone else first.

**Lesson:** If you don't give your best to yourself then don't expect anyone to do it *for* you...it just doesn't work that way. Self-Love, Self-Respect, and Self-Empowerment all begin with *Self* first! It's okay...You can share with the world after you get it together with yourself first.

# DAY 17
## *"I Can Only Be Me!*

You see at the end of the day I will never stop being me.
I will continue to live for me.
Breathe for me.
Work for me.
Play for me.
Believe in me. Die for me.

Even if I don't make YOU happy.

See, the tricky thing is that I really don't know how to be anything or anyone else but myself. And if you can't find "happy" in that, then we cannot co-exist in the same place.

You see, I always know "I am; I can; I will and I do." Despite you.

It doesn't matter if you are my man, my woman, my mother, my father, sister, brother, boss or my friend…I am still only me, and that's what you are going to get.

I am true to myself because I know that my strength lies within in.
That my spirit is full of the stuff that God made me with and that "no man" will take me under.

## Dr. Adair f. White-johnson

My faith is the catalyst for the strengthening of the ivy vine that continuously connects me to my soul. And my determination serves as the springboard that allows me to jump ahead of my own dreams.

There's no "ratchet-ness" over here because I am *THAT* beautiful woman who is "so much" and then again, she is "so much" more.

I have to think for myself to do for myself to love myself and to survive with myself.

My spiritual, emotional and psychological sobriety is just not dependent upon your responses and your requirements of me.

Nah, I can't go out like that.

I'm stronger than that because I really live for me, and I know that God made me as I am because he believes in me.

Am I perfect? Hell naw!

And do I make lots of mistakes? Y'all already know I do.
But none of that stops me from being me.

It's all I got.

And the end of the day when lights are off and it's just me, myself and I am laying in the bed, who am I going to talk to and get "real" answers besides God?

## How to Get Over It in 30 Days Part II

Yeah, that's right…it's only me.

So please, stop trying to change the way I think so you can change the way I behave…

I've got lots of dreams to fulfill, and when one dream is done, I've got many others to go after so I'm empowered, uplifted and inspired…by my own self.

And, it feels good.
Damn good.
I got this.

So please just let me be me and take the time to go and discover your own self…You'll see the difference it will make in your world…

***Lesson:*** Always be yourself despite and in spite of what others try to make of you. Yes, sometimes you will have to "play the game" but never, ever forget that it's just a game and the real truth always comes out when you look into the mirror.

*Dr. Adair f. White-johnson*

# DAY 18
## *"From My Heart"*

After the Jordan Davis verdict, I felt the need to repost this...I wrote it the day after the Trayvon Martin verdict because essentially I feel the same way I did after that verdict was released...And now there is Michael Brown and Eric Garner and so many others...I updated it a bit.

I typically don't post this type of blog, but I've been up since late last night thinking about the outcome of the Trayvon Martin trial and decided to share my thoughts/feelings with all of you....

My 4 Sons....
I have not 1, not 2, not 3, but 4 sons who happen to like Skittles Iced Tea and 'loud" music.

This verdict makes me shiver with fear at this moment because I do not know what kind of future they have to live in a society where cold blooded murder is justified.

I don't think it would matter that my sons benefitted from a private school education, have lived in an upper-middle class neighborhood their entire lives, are active participants in their church, do community service, are excellent scholar-athletes and are basically just plain ol' "good kids."

The bullets that pierce hearts don't know nor do they understand this...it doesn't seem to matter.

## How to Get Over It in 30 Days Part II

You see bullets don't have names on them...They just do what they are supposed to do...Hurt and Kill....But people, we know, we understand, but yet we still pull the trigger so the bullets can Hurt and Kill...

How can this be justified? How can this be rationalized as the "right" thing to do? Does being cloaked in terms such as "stand your ground" make it permissible? Legitimate? Authorized? If you had asked me this a week ago I would have shouted "NO!" but these verdicts have lawfully proven me wrong.

Hmmmm...

What I do know is that I have 4 sons who live and breathe the same air as those who embrace the warped ideology that renegade behavior is synonymous with "self-defense" and I have to teach them to think differently to behave differently because of this.

Remember, we must first change the way we think in order to change the way we behave.

Perhaps the real weapon of destruction was the mindset of these now men...Their prejudicial stances about someone else's son and their obvious overzealous need to be in control of "situations" that really weren't "situations" at all...Just somebody's son walking home with Skittles and Iced Tea...Or sitting in a car listening to "loud" music.

And although I told my husband that I didn't believe the state necessarily presented their case "beyond a reasonable doubt" in one case and did not do a great job in the other, I did believe that somehow, someway, "justice would prevail."

I guess it would have to happen in another place at another time. And I guess the Jordan Davis case wasn't that time either...

But I still have 4 sons, right NOW--TODAY who happen to like Skittles and Iced Tea, wear hoodies and listen to "loud" music all the time....

What type of country are we now living in?

***Lesson:*** Hmmmm...Not sure what it is here.

## DAY 19
## *"God is the only Hercules"*

You are not stronger than God.

No matter how hard you try to make things go in the direction you want them to, God's will always prevail.

You may climb many mountains during your life but God is always waiting for you on the other side because he has pushed all the sharp rocks out of your way and he has passed directly through the actual core of those mountains.

You may feel victorious because you have won many battles in your life, but God provided the artillery you used to win, and he is a champion and always the King.

You may stand courageous by claiming triumph through tragedy, but it was God's shoulders that you stood on for the strength and the tenacity you used to pull yourself through it all.

And you may be satisfied with accepting life "as is" but it was God who ordered your steps and created the life path upon which you travel.

You see although we are already "so much," God is always so much more.

We need to lean continuously on him and his shields of grace, faith, and mercy for guidance.
Know that we are empowered only by his will.
And nourished only by the gifts he has laid on his table for us to feast upon.

We never limit our possibilities.
We don't disable our abilities.
And we can't predict our future capabilities.

Because we know that our God is the only omnipotent one.
We know that we have to let him do his work and teach us how to do our own.
We must let him lead us as we follow in his footsteps.

And we must live with what he has decided for us -- whether we like it or not.

We are not "special" because we have "gone through" some stuff in our lives...We are simply stronger because of it.
But we are never stronger than God because he has been the one who carried us through it all.

***Lesson:*** You never do it alone. You can never be strong without faith in God. You will never be able to "outwit/outsmart" God or even bargain with him to get what you want. It just doesn't work that way. Be accepting and obedient to his Word, and you will find all the strength that you need there.

## DAY 20
### *"Here's What I Know"*

Sometimes I think that when we are broken down to our weakest position that we are the strongest.

It is when we have "nothing" that we notice that we actually have "everything" we need.

When we feel the tears streaming down our faces that we realize that they are not all tears of heartache and pain but are also tears of release...

Release of the pressure in our lives,
Release of the toxins that have been poisoning our minds and
Release of the burdens of the seemingly impossible.

When we are "broken" down, we realize our resiliency in the raw.
We see our strength in the invisible...grace, faith, and mercy.
We feel our omnipotence conquer fear of the unknown.

When our souls are less heavy then, our hearts can be more open.
Because we need them fulfilled and nourished with love as we begin our struggle for significance.

## Dr. Adair f. White-johnson

We search that the laboratory of redemption to discover a cure for our pain and the elements that may cause us to stagnate and hesitate our emotional growth.
We begin our journey of self-discovery by climbing the mountains of revelation and truth.

We travel down roads of uncertainty to recapture dreams deferred.

And we visit pastures to fertilize the grains and foundation of who we really are so that we can grow into that person we aspire to be.

Yes, when we are broken down we may be damaged but we are not destroyed.
It's simply a time when we are taken back to the essence of who we really are and understand how to live in our true purpose of life.

We learn more.
We pray more.
We believe more.
We do more.
We become more.

Going through "stuff" takes us back to the simple things in life...Many of the things that we lose amidst the financial and material success that we may have experienced during our lifetime.

## *How to Get Over It in 30 Days Part II*

We learn to persevere without prized possessions.
And we embrace our positive potential as we prepare
ourselves for when God says "Yes!"

We want to be ready to begin to walk along the path
he created for us and follow the steps he ordered just
for us...without bringing all of that old, hurtful
baggage with us.
To do this, we have to be "stripped" down and
"broken" apart so we can be fully healed.
So that we can love again.
Feel again.
Know again.
And believe again.

And it's hard when we are hurting.
Real hard.
But that's the time when we need to know that the
best is yet to come... That there is no place to go but
"up" because we've hit "rock bottom" and God has
thrown us his rope of faith that we can use to climb
out of that valley of despair.

We can do it.
It's all in the process of renewal.
In the training of unquestionable faith.
And in the workshop of resiliency.
This is what I know.

## Dr. Adair f. White-johnson

***Lesson:*** Sometimes it hurts so bad that we just want to give up and give in. We don't understand why we are going through the challenges...that we don't deserve this struggle...Then we begin to question our faith and doubt our commitment to that faith...WRONG. Know that there has to be pain for joy to exist, and there has to be a challenge before you can claim a victory...It is all part of this circle of life and sometimes it just happens to be "your turn." Keep knowing, keep believing and you will begin to see the positive changes and begin to experience the difference in your life.

## DAY 21
## "Fear Not"

Fear not what you need the most.
Fear not what you want the least.

Sometimes we become afraid of our own dreams
And stagnate our steps to make them a reality.

We create barriers to our own success by what we do and what we fail to do.
We put protective armor around our souls in an effort to shield our hearts from pain
And our spirits from being broken.

But know that as long as you believe that God orders your steps then your dreams can never become your nightmares.

Be prepared that when God says "Yes!" he may take you to places you've never been...

You may travel roads that are not paved, and you may climb mountains yet unnamed.

Those valleys that you stumble upon may cause you to fall down a few times but remember that this is the path that He has chosen for you.

And he has never failed you yet.

## Dr. Adair f. White-johnson

Fear of the unknown should not detour you from following your dreams.
It's what you do already know that will most likely be your alternate route away from greatness.

Your emotional and spiritual sobriety should not be dependent on warped ideas.

But instead should rely on the faith of God's plans for you...

Fear not.
Be not.
Give up not.

Your steps have already been ordered.
What's for you is already for you.
Just be prepared and begin the journey and fear not yourself.

***Lesson:*** Sometimes we are afraid to dream because we are afraid to fail, and we don't clearly understand our destiny. But when God calls you to "do you," be not afraid because he's "got your back." Go for it. Take a chance. Live being who you really are, who God has chosen you to be...That means following those dreams and walking down that uncomfortable road of the unknown. Fear not because God is always by your side.

## DAY 22
### *"Can you hear your Heart?"*

Don't you absolutely hate when people don't listen to you?

When you feel as though you are talking to a wall because no one is responding to your words?

How frustrating is that?

Well, how do you think God feels when you do not listen to his words in your spirit?
When you fail to follow the dreams that he has implanted in your heart?
When you ignore the "signs," the "feelings" and the "opportunities" that are placed before you?

We are often guilty when we stagnate our hopes and abbreviate our goals because we just don't listen to what our spirit tells us.

We limit our possibilities by doubting our abilities.

We fear what we want most and embrace what we need least.

We settle for less, and we accept the least.
And then we think we are happy with the results.
That is definitely not the plan that God has for us.

There is an abundance of joy and happiness in the universe, and you deserve as piece of it but you have to listen to the voice that God has instilled in you.

Don't question his plans for you.
Don't question your purpose that he has created for you.

What's for you is for you.

Your life was designed for greatness, but you first have to listen.
You have to feel what God has placed in your soul to understand your direction that will lead to your destiny.

God's words should not fall upon deaf ears because the "sound" of his voice should resonate in your spirit and order your steps.

It all begins with faith.

I've said this before…you need your faith in order to listen and trust in God.
To know that when he speaks to you, he is speaking to YOU directly, and this is the part where you need to be STILL to listen.
Hearing his voice in your heart will "free" you to walk down that uncomfortable road to greatness and travel along the road less traveled to self-fulfillment.

*How to Get Over It in 30 Days Part II*

Empowering your heart, empowering your soul, empowering your spirit and empowering your dreams all begin with listening to the words that God is saying to you.
You can't ignore him because God doesn't "go away."
You can't "walk away" from him because God is within you -- no matter where you go.
And you can't pretend like he is not there because he is everywhere.

Ah yes, we know that when folks don't listen to what we are saying it is very frustrating and at times disappointing.
But yet we choose to ignore the words that God speaks to us daily.

Stop it. Just stop it.

He knows, and he lets YOU know that the dreams in your soul are there for YOU.

Listen and follow your dreams…
Empower your dreams.
Empower yourself with the knowledge that God is always on your side…

He supports you, and he believes in you and what you can do. He has given you those dreams to make your reality.
And when you finish with one dream he always has another for you to follow.

Be inspired.
Be empowered.
Be still to listen.

***Lesson:*** Being ignored is frustrating, and we often think it doesn't make sense. We want others to listen to us and follow our instructions. Well, in this life you are charged with doing the same thing. Listen to what is in your heart, don't ignore the "signs" and follow the "drive" in your soul to achieve all of your goals. After all, it is God speaking to you…and when he speaks, we must all stop to listen.

## Day 23
### *"Helplessness"*

The other day I was caught up in the Atlanta "snowcapolypse" debacle and stuck in the traffic with two of my boys for 10 hours.

Tired. Hungry. Stressed. Terrified and exasperated are only a few of the adjectives I could use to describe my feelings during that time.

The biggest emotion that I felt was just "Helplessness."

This was simply an emotion that I am never comfortable with...
I've always been that girl who "makes" things happen and not just "let" things happen in my life...
Always in control.

So when my large SUV spun around on an icy hill the total feeling of helplessness was somewhat foreign to me....

What do you do when you feel helpless?
How do you respond?
Do you respond?

The only thing I knew how to do was to pray.
Be still and pray.

## Dr. Adair f. White-johnson

After taking control over my truck again, I decided to get it over to a nearby gas station where we simply stopped everything we were thinking and doing and just prayed.

My 12-year-old asked God to wrap his arms around us to protect us and to cloak us with his strength so we would feel mentally and emotionally strong enough to get back on the road again.

The 10-year-old asked that God reveal the shields we needed to lean on to "help us get home."

And I prayed that instead of feeling helpless that God granted me the power to feel hopeful again so I could deliver us home safely.

You see, after driving 8 hours so far I was feeling weak...Mentally, physically, and somewhat spiritually because I didn't see the movement on the streets that I wanted to.

I felt like I was losing faith, and I forgot to pray.

I forgot that my God was the one really in control and that he had already ordered my steps.
As I tried just to use my mind to help me figure out how to "fix" this I forgot to use my heart and my spirit to lead and guide me.

So deciding to pull into a gas station allowed me to refuel, re-energize and rejuvenate --- my Spirit.

## *How to Get Over It in 30 Days Part II*

Eventually, the boys and I were able to make it home safely but I was reminded of a few things that day...

1. If faith can move mountains, it can surely move you too. Hold on to it because it will be that shield you need to lean on when needed. If you allow fear to paralyze your faith then, you will never be able to walk again.

2. Sometimes we just have to let people love us.
We have to let them help us.
We have to let them believe in us.
And we have to let them pray for us.
You see, being that "superwoman" or "go-to-guy" can be a lonely and isolated position when we end up in the same position that we were originally started in. No matter how hard we try.
We begin to think that we can
Do it all.
Handle it all.
Fix it all.
Transform it all.
Without anyone else.
And without "letting to and letting God."
Wrong.
This won't work.
We need to be loved and taken care of so that we can love and continue to take care of others too.
But we have to allow it.
We have to remember "prayer changes everything" so accept them from others.

During this crisis, I needed to allow my husband to venture out to try and find us to help. Although I initially thought it was best he remained home I had to allow him to love and protect us the best way he knew how...Even if it meant he risked his own life driving on the ice to reach us.

3. Trust in God. Know that no matter how scared, confused and frustrated you are, filling your heart with God's love can only make you feel better, stronger and more capable.
Pulling into that gas station and praying with my boys allowed me to reclaim what I thought I lost during my crisis.
I became better, stronger and more faithful for it because I recognized that what is "God's will" is not always "Man's way" but I needed to listen to what God had to say...

Feeling helpless is still not a favorite emotion of mine but now I am ready for it...I have my weapon of mass destruction--my faith. And I plan to use it the next time the world is spinning around, and I'm ready to just "jump off."

## How to Get Over It in 30 Days Part II

***Lesson:*** Life can be rough sometimes and we feel a range of negative emotions---sometimes our faith and trust in God gets mixed up in our hurt, fear and confusion and we forget to just stop, be still and pray. But we have to. Somehow, some way, despite and in spite we have to touch our hearts with the Word of God---once we feel him within us then our spirits will be refueled and we will be ready to get up and begin again. Believing that prayer changes everything makes you understand that you are never really "helpless" after all.

## DAY 24
## *"Hide and Seek"*

Okay, I'm going to need you to come out from hiding in that dark place.

I'm going to need you to come from hiding from your fears.

Hiding from your pain.
Hiding from your past.
Hiding from yourself.

God has his hands on you, and he touches you all over and it will be alright.

He is a God of second chances.

I'm going to need you to come out and enter that laboratory of redemption.

You may be damaged, but you are not destroyed.

Just because you have "been through some stuff" in your life doesn't make you special...It only makes you hurt because of it.

But despite and in spite of it you can still live in your true purpose and sing in your own choir of joy and happiness.
But I'm gonna need you to "Let Go and Let God" first.

## How to Get Over It in 30 Days Part II

You are going to have to "Get Over It!" before you can begin traveling down that uncomfortable road to reclaiming and rejuvenating your spirit...

That takes faith, commitment, truth, and resiliency.

These are already in you...You just need to trust and believe that you can pull them out of you.

Reject the cycle of spiritual, emotional and psychological poverty that you have conditioned yourself to.

And reject the mental enslavement of defeat that you have sold your mind into.

It's all about mind over matter.
If you don't mind then it shouldn't matter.
I'm gonna need you to understand that the change really does begin with you.

Change your heart.
Change your level of faith.
Change your mind.
Change your life.
And sometimes that means changing some of the folks around you.

So release yourself from that jail of loneliness, despair, doubt and low self-esteem so you can begin to live in a world that is enriched, fulfilling and prosperous.

A world that already embraces who you really are doesn't limit your possibilities and disable your abilities.

You got this.

You really do.

So I'm gonna need you come out from hiding...Let us see the "real" you...The good, the bad and even the "ugly." --Past sins, past lies and past mistakes...

We need to "see" it all so we can help you begin walking on your path of redemption, forgiveness and positive change in your life.

Despite and in spite of it all...

***Lesson:*** Life is not a game of "hide and seek" because all you can do is "run" and never really "hide" from yourself...Every time you look in the mirror, the same reflection will be staring back at you. And mirrors don't lie.

# DAY 25
## *Here's What I Know:*

When your world feels like everything is crumbling around you, remember just to lean on those shields that you cannot see.

The shield of *FAITH* --knowing that God has ordered your steps, and everything will eventually be alright because God has paved the road that you will travel on.

The shield of *HOPE* --knowing that tomorrow is only a day away, so positive changes are always possible.

The shield of *MERCY* --knowing that if you turn it all over to God, remain thankful and trust in him then the best is yet to come.

The shield of *HUMILITY*-- knowing that you are NOT greater, stronger, wiser and better than God's will. Being obedient and accepting his Word will allow you to see beyond today's situation and know with God's blessings you own the power of change.

You see I know that life can be hard and that sometimes when we awaken in the morning we just want to roll over and go back to sleep because we immediately feel the heartache and pain that we ended yesterday with.

We don't want to get out of the bed because we know that we still don't have the answers to the problems that we went to bed with last night---
We want just to roll back over and fade into a deep sleep where we can dream about how our lives "should" be.

It just feels better that way.

But we can't stay in the bed all day and every day.

We must rise to face our challenges, acknowledge our struggles for significance and embrace that there are some days that will begin and end without any answers.

So yes, sometimes we feel as though our world is crumbling around us, and there isn't much we can do about it...

But remember that we all own the power of prayer and the knowledge that "prayer changes everything" so we can't "give" up and we must "get" up to live in our purpose each day...

**Lesson:** Life can be "rough" for many days, and we may feel that there is "no way out," but know that you always have an opening...Leaning on your shields of faith, hope, mercy, and humility as your weapons of mass destruction of negativity in your life are those openings. Become that warrior of strength and foot soldier emerging from the trenches of despair because you know that God "has your back" and somehow, someway, "every lil' thing will be alright..."

# DAY 26
## *"It Never was Lost"*

Sometimes we look too hard to "find ourselves" when we were never really lost in the first place.

We search for our inner beings,
Our thoughts.
Our voices.
And our feelings.

But all the while they haven't really been anywhere at all.
They've just been tucked under layers of doubt, confusion, hurt, disappointment, bewilderment, disillusion, anger, dissatisfaction.

And we think we can no longer see them, feel them and know them.
We think that we are always entitled to clarity and transparency in our lives.

And that things should not require intellectual and emotional focus.
Instead, it should all be "easy."

We just need to begin the process of removing the layers to find what we have been desperately searching for.
And then we will realize that it was still there all along.

## Dr. Adair f. White-johnson

We'll find our strength beneath our fears...
Once we "let go and let God."

We'll find our happiness once we release our pain.
We'll find ways to forgive others once we have mastered forgiving ourselves.
We'll find success once we recognize how to learn from our failures.
We'll find love once we know how to give love.

We'll find self-empowerment once we relinquish any commitments to the mental enslavement of mediocrity.
We'll discover the depths of our souls when we find the breadth of our spirits.

And we will find strength once we understand our struggle for significance.

We just need to learn how to be "still."
We just need to learn how to be "obedient" to God's Word.
And we just need to learn to trust ourselves to trust in God.

Let me say it again...

*"We just need to learn to trust ourselves to trust in God."*

*How to Get Over It in 30 Days Part II*

Once we are secure with leaning on our shields grace, faith, mercy and God, whatever we have been searching for will be revealed to us.

And we'll discover that it has never really been lost at all.

***Lesson:*** Everything you need and all that you are is already within you. You just have to look behind the mask you may be wearing.

## DAY 27
## *Here's What I Know:*

Sometimes I think we forget how powerful we really are...

We forget the magnificent characteristics that God has bestowed upon us.

The power of our MIND that allow us to think about situations and our lives differently so we can analyze, synthesize and evaluate before making choices.

The power of HOPE so we can continue feeling and believing that positive changes are coming because God orders our steps and we are traveling along the path he created for us.

The power of FAITH because we know that although we can't see God's strength we feel it in everything we do so that empowers us to believe more so we can do more.

The power of RESILIENCY that enables us to continue our daily battles with life challenges, broken hearts, troubled relationships and questionable financial stability. With resiliency, we know that we are able to "bounceback" after hitting rock bottom and that although we may be "damaged" we are never "destroyed."

*How to Get Over It in 30 Days Part II*

The power of LOVE so we can feel as though we belong, accepted, appreciated, wanted, respected and committed.

The power of PERSEVERANCE that motivates us to keep trying, to stand strong through adversity, to continue fighting for our place in the world and to not give up in our struggle for significance as we travel "up" on "down" escalators.

We are destined for greatness, and we have been blessed with PERSEVERANCE to ensure that we can withstand the trials and tribulations of life to reach our pinnacles of happiness.

The power of CHANGE so that if we feel as though we lost all of the above we can still remember that we own the power of CHANGE and the option to "fix it" so we can become "whole" again and make a difference in our own lives...Never allowing ourselves to become mentally enslaved to negative thoughts that limit our possibilities.

Yes, we are supreme people with magical powers that will allow us to create our happy worlds...
We just have to remember how to "wave our wands" to motivate, inspire and empower our lives.

***Lesson***: God has bestowed upon us the power we need to be happy. But it's our responsibility to know how to use those powers to strengthen our daily lives.

*Dr. Adair f. White-johnson*

# DAY 28
## *Here's What I Know:*

When I walked away from a six-figure income a couple of years ago to follow my dreams and live in my purpose, I knew that I also walked towards self-fulfillment.

When I turned my back on trying to achieve total happiness through financial security, I also knew that my back was now facing the misery and tension that threatened my happiness in the six-figure positions.

I knew that I wanted more.
Needed more.
And could be more.
I understood that my jobs really didn't define who I am.

And all that I was destined to be.
So I took a chance and walked away.
Stepping out on faith.
Leaning on the shields of grace, mercy, and humility.

And knowing that the best was yet to come.
I was preparing for when God was ready to say "YES!"
Preparing for the moment when I had the strength to travel down the uncomfortable road of the unknown.

# How to Get Over It in 30 Days Part II

To face my fears of the future.
And to embrace my destiny.
Was I scared when I walked away from the comfort and security of the position that I had known for my entire adult life?

Hell yes!

But I was more afraid of what would happen to my dreams if I didn't.

I was afraid for my heart; each day it was becoming more unfulfilled as it marinated in misery while in that professional position.

I was terrified that I was becoming that person who "shoulda, woulda, coulda" been, but simply wasn't.

And I was scared of the person I was becoming because of the empty professional relationships I existed in.

It wasn't worth it.
So I walked away.

And I ran to my dreams.
My future.
My happiness.
My destiny.
My purpose.

## Dr. Adair f. White-johnson

And I'm better for it.
Stronger because of it.
And more magnificent living in it.
You see, dreams don't come with a warranty or guarantee so it is up to you to work a dream to live the dream.
You are responsible for following your own dreams.

And remembering that God orders your steps...not man.

Knowing this requires that sometimes you have to make unpopular choices and personal sacrifices to achieve those dreams.

But at the end of the day when you are laying in your bed, alone with your thoughts, you will know that it was all worth it.

You will know that money cannot buy true happiness and the last time I checked, dreams weren't for sale anywhere either...

I learned that a while ago, so I walked away from a six-figure income and walked towards my true life and my ultimate happiness.

Yes, dreams can come true...

But remember the work to make them happen is still up to you...

***Lesson:*** Money doesn't dictate appiness...Following dreams do.

## DAY 29
## *Here's What I Know:*

Some of us claim that we have adopted a "Let Go and Let God" philosophy to lead our lives but yet we want to "pick and choose" what we are going to "give" God to handle.

We often decide to only "allow" him to salvage the "messes" that we make and conquer any adversity that we may face.

We convince ourselves that we are people who are empowered and not enslaved so we are able-bodied and "strong" enough to handle what life has to offer so we don't share the battles with God until we feel we are losing the war.

You see, because we are self-confident some of our behaviors reek of arrogance...
As though we know it all, been through it all and done it all at least three times.

We believe that our knowledge combined with our experience are the only guided tools we need to push us through the pain and make us feel good again....

So, we don't call on God until it hurts.
And hurts real bad.

And we realize that we can't do it alone...not by ourselves...we are now afraid and fear breeds confusion and doubt so we know that we need Jesus and we need him now so that's when we decide to "Let Go and Let God."

Hmmmmmm....

What if we gave God the power and the glory for each and everything that we do daily?

Suppose we shared the emotional and psychological poverty with him from the beginning?

Suppose we prayed that he would wrap his arms around us and hold us tight every day, so we are cloaked in his love and strength?

Suppose we did this so his omnipotence would flow through us, and we can feel his power in everything that we do....running through us like nutrients in our bloodstreams?

What if we simply "believed" in the power of Prayer and what God can and will do for us whether we like it or not?

See, I believe that God does have all the "extra" pieces we need to complete our life puzzles but we spend way too much time trying to figure it out ourselves...One piece at a time.

## How to Get Over It in 30 Days Part II

Yes, I am that "strong woman" and I think I can do it all but I know that I can do nothing, be nothing and achieve nothing with God's imprint on my life.
He orders my steps and through triumph and tragedy he is a shield that I lean on....

When you "Let Go and Let God" you're letting him into your entire life....
You are not simply "picking and choosing" because God is not a Choice.

He is real, and he is a requirement to make it through daily....

To "Let Go and Let God" means "letting him in."
Let him into your decisions, your hopes, your dreams, your goals, your success and your failure...

He'll enjoy being there because he loves you....
Anyway.

Despite and In spite of everything.

***Lesson:*** Trust and believe so that so you can "Let Go and Let God...." He knows what you are doing anyway so why not?

*Dr. Adair f. White-johnson*

# DAY 30
## *Here's What I Know:*

Sometimes when we are missing something in our lives we go searching for the wrong things in all the wrong places.

And when we search, we search hard.
With a purpose.

But still in the wrong places and looking for the wrong stuff.

We look for square bandages to fill circular holes
And we try to replace triangular emotions with rectangular promises of love.

But we end up confused.
And go right back searching while listening to the sounds of what used to be "silent tears."

Doing it this way we will never allow us to Get Over It!

Instead, we just end up putting those band-aids on gunshot wounds.
And then sit and watch our hearts and souls bleed again.
We try to replace one love with another.
And we forget that love ain't like batteries...You just can't replace one with another.

## How to Get Over It in 30 Days Part II

So then we wonder why the new love can't fix the old love and fill that void in our hearts and that empty spot in our souls...

See, you can only heal if you allow yourself to strip those emotions to the raw, reach your core and peel off those layers of pseudo-strength and courage.

Open your hearts to allow them to breathe so the pain will suffocate and eventually die.

You'll never know what your emotional and psychological sobriety is dependent upon if you are always intoxicated with old hurts...

You've got to get over it, get through it and keep it moving to begin to fill voids in our lives with positivity and promise.

Look at the holes as the foundation of your life that must be filled...

If you fill it with sponges soaked with hatred, it will only absorb more hatred and cannot carry your weight.

If you fill it with cotton it will be too soft and you'll be hurt over and over again.

And if you only pour cement into all the cracks and crevices within you then you will be hardened to all the love that is destined to come your way.

But if you begin to fill your void with faith, confidence, courage, resilience, humility, spirituality and other characteristics of positivity your foundation will be solid and you will be able to stand strong and begin to truly heal.

So yes, we often try to fill our voids with "stuff" just so we can Get Over It! but if we use the "wrong stuff" then our lives become more complicated and the results more devastating.

And then we are right back where we started from.

Hurt.

***Lesson:*** Be sure that when you are healing that you heal from the "inside out" so that you don't try to use the "wrong stuff" to help you through the process. Your heart, soul, and spirit are not exchangeable so don't try to swap them out just to Get Over It!

# DAY 31
## *Here's What I Know:*

This morning I decided at the last minute that I wanted to get my hair "done." I wanted it to be shampooed and styled by a professional because they do such a better job than I can.

Knowing that my "regular" stylist would be unavailable at the last minute, I decided to go to my "backup" salon.

As the stylist began shampooing my hair, I thought about how good it felt; she was scrubbing and massaging my scalp and the sensation just felt good...I was relaxed with my eyes closed and kept thinking "she is really scrubbing, and it was wonderful!"

Well, it continued to feel good until the third time that she began scrubbing...by this time my scalp felt tender...almost raw...Each time that I felt her fingers on my scalp it felt like daggers digging into my skin. No longer was I smiling and relaxed...Instead, what used to feel so good now felt painful...It was hurting me...

But why didn't I tell her?
Why didn't I let her know that she was hurting me?
That this wasn't "fun" anymore?
That I wanted her to STOP?

## Dr. Adair f. White-johnson

Was it because I felt I deserved it because I chose to come to this salon?

Or was it because I felt I needed it so my hair could be beautiful at the end of the experience?

Why would I allow anyone to inflict any amount of pain on me and tell myself that it was okay?

Hmmmmm.....

Now let's parallel this to the way some of us live our lives...

We allow heartache and pain to take up residence in our lives and then convince ourselves that it is okay.

We don't tell them to STOP...

We already know that it doesn't feel good when someone we love deliberately hurts us and is unapologetic for it but yet we remain in that same situation.

Still convincing ourselves that we deserved it or that it will get better with a little more time...

Or, that we don't have another choice.

Hmmmmm....

## How to Get Over It in 30 Days Part II

In many instances remaining in an emotionally, psychologically and physically abusive relationship may be a choice in itself...

You choose to be more afraid of the unknown in the world if you left the situation than you are afraid of the actual situation. We allow fear to paralyze our thought process and immobilize our ability to move towards change.

You choose just to build more walls and barriers around your heart and soul instead of creating plans about how to just totally demolish the negative situation that is hurting you.

You choose to deny your faith that will ultimately lead you and guide you along the path that God has created for you...not the path that this situation has led you on.

And you choose to let them keep hurting you because you choose to remain in the situation.

You see, we are only treated the way we allow ourselves to be treated and we own the power of change. But when we decide to use that power is aligned with the choices we make...We can choose to remain in a toxic situation, or we choose to embrace a new beginning.

So why do we continue to allow ourselves to be hurt?

## Dr. Adair f. White-johnson

In some instances, it's because it's easier...Other times it's because we really have faith in the situation, and we think it's going to work out....

But the faith should be with God and not with man...God paves your road...not the actions of others...
And I already know it's hard to admit to yourself that you are really in pain, that your heart is broken and that you are in this situation and you feel "stuck" thinking "No way! This is not happening to ME!"

But accepting what it is and what it means is one of the first steps to moving towards peace...to not hurt anymore.

So as the stylist was finishing my hair I realized that my scalp was no longer sore, my skin actually felt rejuvenated, and I was pleased with the outcome.

BUT!!! Washing hair is not synonymous with washing away pain!

Pain just doesn't dissolve like bubbles and soap. And may not be temporary and rinsed out either.

It has to be taken care of...it cannot be ignored because unlike the shampooing of hair it doesn't disappear and get better within 30 minutes.

## How to Get Over It in 30 Days Part II

If left unattended it could hurt for an entire lifetime...that's one of the reasons why so many people walk around with antiquated pain bottled up inside...they never said *STOP!* so it only fermented over the years and is now attached to their hearts...

Begin to say *STOP!* to people who hurt you.

Say *STOP!* to yourself for allowing the hurt to continue in your life.

And say *STOP!* to the situations that bring you pain...

It's the only way to begin the process to "Get Over It!"

**Lesson:** Sometimes you have to STOP! before you can GO!

Dr. Adair f. White-johnson

# "After 30 Days"

## *Do you need a "little more?"*

This remainder of this book provides you with additional empowering messages "just because."

*How to Get Over It in 30 Days Part II*

## *Here's What I Know:*

Sometimes we hurt so badly that we don't know where to begin in our healing process.

All we know is that we want the pain to disappear...to free us so we can live and love again.

We want to feel "normal" so we can function "pain-free."

We just want the hurt to go away.

And we are willing to do almost anything to make it happen...Fast.

So we begin to take quick ways out to feel better...

We mask our pain with fake happiness; we fill the holes in our hearts with useless and destructive relationships, and we pretend that everything is "alright" and "we got this."

 But the pain is still there.
And it hurts.

You see you can't just put a Band-Aid on a gunshot wound and expect it to heal by itself.
It needs surgery.
And you can't just wish your pain away and expect it to heal either.

Just because you can't see it doesn't mean it doesn't exist because you can still feel it.

And it still hurts.

Beginning the road to emotional recovery is not going to be easy but you have to be true to yourself...

You can start the process by doing the following things:

    1. Step out of the "denial" zone and admit that you are hurt.

    2. Realize the true source of your pain...don't camouflage it with excuses...What really happened and why? Focus on determining if you are hurt because your heart is broken, your ego diminished, your expectations are not met, etc. You really have to figure out *WHY* you are hurting before you can begin to heal...

    3. Know your role in your pain...What did you do or didn't do that could have contributed to your pain?

    4. Ask yourself if you really want to get over the pain...Some folks find it easier to live in a "comfortable hell" than to fight to live in an "uncomfortable heaven."

    5. Pray. Prayer changes everything and everyone. Just do it.

## How to Get Over It in 30 Days Part II

I don't like to hurt because it hurts.
It's simple.

I want to work to make that hurt disappear...

Fast.

But you have to make your own decision...Do you want to heal truly?

Are you ready to do the surgery for your emotional recovery?

Be honest...

In this situation, the truth will really "set you free" and you can become an active agent in your own liberation from heartache and pain.

***Lesson:*** You have to decide if you want release your pain. No one can determine that for you. Once you choose to not hurt anymore the healing process can begin.

*Dr. Adair f. White-johnson*

## *Here's What I Know:*

Sometimes when you hit "rock bottom" and there is no place to go, but "up" be careful about what you stand on when you are climbing...

What may appear as a "boulder" may actually be a hard surface ready to crumble and what may look like a "pebble" may be the only source of strength you need.

***Lesson:*** Don't always depend on those you think should obviously be your support system---they can fail you too.

*How to Get Over It in 30 Days Part II*

# *Here's What I Know:*

*YES!!!!!!*

I deserve it!

I deserve to be happy.
I deserve to be smart.
I deserve to be my kind of cute.
And I deserve to be my kind of strong.

I deserve to be able to say "NO!" and mean it.
And "YES!" when I want to.

I deserve to follow my dream, work my dream so I can live my dream.

And I deserve to dream some more if I want to.

I deserve to own the power in my life and the strength to execute that power in my decisions.

I deserve to be loved...in a good ol' fashioned kind of way.

And I deserve a piece of all the joy and happiness that is abundant in the universe.

I deserve never to limit my possibilities and not disable my abilities.

I deserve to be spiritually free and not mentally enslaved by negative thinking.

I deserve to remove the shackles of shame from any past mistakes because I know better and will do better.

I deserve to know how to be honest with myself so I can be truthful in my choices.

I deserve to know how I really feel about "things" without being pressured to feel certain ways.

I deserve to be drunk with passion...
About my dreams.

And I deserve to be high...About my life.

I deserve the best that I work for.
And I deserve to "do me."

Yeah, I deserve pleasure...without the pain that may come before it.

I deserve to Get Over It.
I deserve to Get Through It.
I deserve to choose to Keep it Moving too...
I deserve to believe in it.
I deserve to receive it.

I deserve it.
So, I'm taking it.
Just because I deserve it.

***Lesson:*** Sometimes you just gotta "take" what is yours because you deserve it. Just because you deserve it.

*How to Get Over It in 30 Days Part II*

## *Here's What I Know:*

So today is the last day of the year...

Hmmmm....

What does that mean to you in your life?

Some of us will struggle with moving into the future because we are holding on to the past---

Clinching to emotions that we claim makes us feel better.
And holding people captive in relationships with us that are not working.

Some of us will be too quick to move into the future...

Running away from the truth in our lives
And trying to escape things and people who force us to make difficult choices to move toward making positive changes in our lives.

We would rather exist in that "comfortable hell" than challenge ourselves to live in an "uncomfortable heaven."

So we run.

And we expect the New Year to "fix" things.

The New Year should reflect new beginnings, new perspectives, new foci, new starts, new hopes and new dreams.

It doesn't mean that you reject everything in your past...

Or, accept it all because it is "new."

It just means that it's a New Year with new possibilities.

So as you plan your resolutions and "bucket" lists be mindful of what you have done, what you failed to do and what you plan to do.

Know your heart and know what's for you is already for you.

Remember that God has already ordered your steps and the path you intend to follow in the New Year should lead you down his road.

Yes, the New Year can mean so many different things to so many people but don't expect to change your life miraculously at the stroke of midnight just because you want it to.

***Lesson:*** Bringing in the New Year is definitely an exciting time because we know that the future is closer to us. We have to be mindful though each new day will be the same as the last if WE don't make a difference.

*How to Get Over It in 30 Days Part II*

## *Letter to a Friend:*

There will always be things about the physical self that you wish you could change, but really can't unless you pay someone to do it for you.

I've always wanted bigger boobs and a bigger butt but even after giving birth to 4 boys I still wear a size 2 without the gift of and "hourglass" shape.

But that doesn't stop me from dreaming and living and enriched and healthy life.

You see, you have to disintegrate the toxins in your life that consistently poison your ability to work your dream to live your dream.

You have to recognize those "tangible" objects that you have the ability to change, but you stagnate on implementing the change.

Negative attitudes.
Negative mindsets.
Faulty dreams.
Faulty reality.
Lazy initiative.
Lazy motivation.
Denial.
Anger. Sadness. Grief. Hopelessness.
Unrealistic expectations.
Low self-esteem and Low self-worth.

Since you own the power of change, you can begin the transformative process.

Begin to know that underneath all of those layers of self-doubt there lies a confident and industrious individual who is destined for greatness.

Know that change always begins and ends with self.

It's based on your viewpoint of yourself and how you fit into the world.

It's like "mind over matter," as much as you "mind," will be as much as it "matters."
And if you don't "mind" then it won't "matter."

My friend, know that you are responsible for your personal growth and transition.
You are responsible for assessing the value of who you are.
You are responsible for determining the value of others in your life.
And you are responsible for loving yourself enough to let the negativity go out of your life.

And is this easy?
Heck no!
But it is necessary for you to be happy.

You will never be happy knowing you haven't tried to make changes.

## How to Get Over It in 30 Days Part II

And you will never be happy accepting every change in your life that is made by someone else.

So it's time to move towards creating your own blueprint of your life --

It's time to follow those steps that God has ordered for you and begin to abandon the destructive self-made path that you've been traveling on ---The path filled with negativity and the unnecessary self-doubt.

It's a great time to begin with a new approach to your life.

Begin thinking about the changes that you can do immediately.
Then plan the transitions that can take place with a few adjustments soon.

And then begin creating the master plan for those things that change your entire life.

Finally, "Just Do It."

Yes, my friend, it's time to make changes so you can feel stronger, healthier, wiser, empowered, motivated and inspired.

But that change first begins with you.

*Dr. Adair f. White-johnson*

***Lesson:*** A New Year can mean a New You. But only if you allow change into your life. Remember, YOU own the power of change, and you must first change the way you think before you can change the way you behave.

*How to Get Over It in 30 Days Part II*

## *Here's What I Know:*

I know that there are a lot of people who are hurt.

> Angry.
> Confused.
> Lost.
> Fearful.
> Ashamed.
> Regretful.
> And many who feel unloved.

But that doesn't have to be you.

You don't have to accept feeling less worthy than you really are because you own the power of change.

You don't have to allow people in your life who do not uplift your spirit, empower your dreams and inspire your motivation.

You own the power to choose who you love AND allow them to be a part of your life.

You see, you don't have to be that person -- that "provocative victim" who only attracts negative elements/people and then become surprised and confused when you are hurt.

You don't have to be that lost soul who seeks to fill your insides with anything that takes up space. And then wonder why you are still unfulfilled.

## Dr. Adair f. White-johnson

If you fill yourself up with nonsense then, that's what your life becomes. Nonsense. Garbage in = Garbage out.

And you don't have to love just anything because you want to love something. That's how you end up with nothing.

You deserve more.
And you can get more.

Stop letting people close enough to you so they can cut your throat...Choke the senses out of you so you cannot inhale positive air and suffocate you with toxic fumes that surround your life.

Stop having charitable sales and auctions to give away your self-value and self-esteem to the lowest bidder so that all you are left with are the characteristics that nobody wants anyway.

And stop surrounding yourself with folks who can't believe in you because they don't even believe in themselves. They can't do anything for you but bring you more misery and false hope.

And yeah, I know you've been through some stuff in your life, and it hurts...I get it.

But you're not "special" because of it.

We all have been through things, and some of us have been through more than others but we still do not receive special awards because of it...

## *How to Get Over It in 30 Days Part II*

So let that go-- It's not a reason to swim in the same pool of self-doubt and self-hate and expect to be happy.

There is so much more of you that is good and positive.

So much more of you that can do great things.
So much more of you that can live and work your dreams.

And so much more of you to be happy.

But you first have to believe it.

And that starts with knowing what's good in your life.
Understanding what makes you feel good.
Knowing what makes you smile.
And claiming those blessings that God has sent to you.

Do it.

Just a little each day and you will begin to see the changes as you look into the mirror and in the way you approach your life.

You deserve it.

Dr. Adair f. White-johnson

***Lesson:*** You don't have to be miserable and unhappy. Sadness is not a terminal illness. And the loneliness can be cured. You are eligible to be loved in a healthy way and deserve to have dreams too. Claim it all and work to make the transition to happiness. You own the power of change...Use it.

*How to Get Over It in 30 Days Part II*

# *Here's What I Know:*

Sometimes it's time to check your "row" to see who is pulling and who is pushing.

Time for you to discover who actually is helping you to row towards your dreams....

If they are pushing while you are pulling,
If they are paddling left when you are steering right,
Or if they are simply not rowing at all and just "sailing along" in your canoe,
Then it's time that they are thrown overboard.

***Lesson:*** There is no tenure in the row if folks are not believing, working and supporting you ---You just can't do life alone and you don't need the "dead weight" on your row to "slow your roll." If you don't clearly decide on the strength of your row team then, you could end up capsizing and eventually drown in your own dreams...

Dr. Adair f. White-johnson

## *Here's What I Know:*

If it doesn't feel uncomfortable or it doesn't hurt then you are probably not trying your hardest.

If you are not second-guessing your next move then, you are probably not doing new things.

If you already know the answers to your own questions then you've probably been in the same place for a long time.

And if your dreams only appear at night then you've probably lost some faith in becoming "more" than what you already are.

You see to make changes in our lives we must think differently to act differently.
And we must feel different to do different things.
We own the power of change.
And we possess the strength to make a change.
We just have to do the work to do it.

Push ourselves through our own self-imposed limits...
Force ourselves to have paradigm shifts ---altering our perspectives of the world.
Allowing ourselves fo approach life and situations from a new angle.
Teaching ourselves to walk up a mountain with the same tenacity that we have when we run down the hill.

## How to Get Over It in 30 Days Part II

Knowing that if we feel comfortable in our current life then we haven't made changes.
That perhaps we haven't required ourselves to define our destiny.
Or we have limited our possibilities.

You see, pushing ourselves to our breaking points is not supposed to be easy...
We pushing for a "break-through" and not a "break-down."
We are supposed to feel our own transformations...
Those changes within ourselves for ourselves.

And just because it doesn't feel good doesn't make it bad...It just means that your soul is working and that change is taking place.

It's the time when we learn that if we know better then we will do better...
And if we do better; then we become better for ourselves.

Yes, if you don't feel it then you are probably not working hard enough...
And if you are not working hard enough then you really should ask yourself if you wanted "it" at all to begin with...

*Dr. Adair f. White-johnson*

***Lesson:*** Achieving your optimal level of success can be a painful process --- You may shed some tears and sweat it out but that's just a normal part of the journey to reach your highest level of performance...Prepare yourself for this workout and know that anything worth having should also be worth fighting and sweating for...You need this to "Get Over It, Get Through It and Keep it Moving."

*How to Get Over It in 30 Days Part II*

## *Here's What I Know:*

There's something about loving yourself that makes you feel whole.

There's something about trusting yourself that makes you feel honest.

There's something about believing in yourself that makes you feel that dreams can come true.

And there's something about thanking God for creating you just as you are that makes you feel special.

So why do always forget these things?

See sometimes we don't embrace how beautiful we are, how smart we are, and we focus on the things we are not.

We don't think about all the good we have done but can quickly write a list of all the wrong we have a part of.

And we don't remember that we are important, and we deserve more because we have trained ourselves to settle for less.

Why is it so hard for us to be good to ourselves?

## Dr. Adair f. White-johnson

We wrap our hearts around other people first and then we try to love ourselves with whatever is left.
 But that's not enough.

Our souls need more to give more.
Our spirits require more to share more.
And our emotional well-being thrives on positivity to become more.

But if we always neglect who we are to focus on what we think we should be then how do we appreciate the person who we live with today?

I know we all strive to accomplish things in our lives but sometimes we just need to be STILL.
We need to listen to the voices within.
And feel the strength of our inner selves...

We can love ourselves stronger this way.

And know that we really are independent, free-spirited, priceless and honest...Enough to love ourselves to "infinity and beyond."

When was the last time that you looked in the mirror and said "I Love You!"?

Hmmmm....

But yet we tell others every day.
And we show them in so many ways.

## How to Get Over It in 30 Days Part II

You see if we don't love ourselves, affirm ourselves and commit to ourselves then how do we empower ourselves?

If we don't pay more attention to ourselves and to who we really are then at some point when we look into that mirror again we will be staring at an empty reflection...at a person that never really was.

Yeah, there's just something about lovin' yourself that makes you stronger...And makes you happy to be you so much longer...

***Lesson:*** Don't forget to love yourself first...You have to love you, trust you, believe in you and empower you before you are any good to anyone else.

*Dr. Adair f. White-johnson*

## *Here's What I Know:*

Sometimes changing the way you think is just so damn hard.

Your heart wants to, but your mind plays tricks on you and makes you believe that you can't.

When you want to be "out" of love with someone because it's "just time" and you feel like you love them longer and harder you feel so weak.

And when you want to change that job because it just doesn't meet your needs anymore you feel so scared of what the future may bring.

And changing the way you think about certain situations so you can maintain relationships and "peace" in your life seems like a daunting task.

So you second guess yourself.

You want to do the right thing, so you pray for guidance.
You want to feel the right thing, so you pray for inspiration.
But yet, it is just so damn hard.

See changing the way we think requires a shift in our ideological, philosophical, spiritual and emotional paradigms.

## How to Get Over It in 30 Days Part II

Ideological, philosophical, spiritual and emotional paralysis can have the worst impact than physical paralysis.
If you don't feel anything in your heart and your soul and you don't use your brain then you have paralyzed your ability to live a happy life...you can live a fulfilled life with a physical paralysis but I'm not convinced that you can do it if you are living with a spiritual paralysis.

It demands we acknowledge that our greatest strengths may also be our greatest weaknesses.

And it requires our resiliency in the raw.
We have to reject failure as an option.
And embrace success as the only solution.

We need to want the mindset change so badly that we are willing to change our lifestyle and our "life-beings" because of it.

We have to remove the layers of fear, anguish, despair, doubt, shame and "fakeness" to begin to change our minds to live healthier lifestyles. This is all the stuff our change gets caught up in.

Remember that just like that bucket of water that can be eventually filled with one drop at a time, your mindset can shift with one thought at a time...
Healthy minds lead to healthy behavior which takes us down the path to a healthy life.

## Dr. Adair f. White-johnson

Is it hard? Uhhh, YEAH!

It is easier to live in that "comfortable hell" than to strive for existence in an "uncomfortable heaven" so we settle to remain in the mindset that we've always had.

We are so afraid…we have that fear of the unknown and that "drama-free" zone that we don't allow ourselves to grow and become what we are destined to be. But dreams don't come with a warranty or guarantee so we need to change our thought process to achieve them.

There is no "master" plan to change our minds ….We simply begin by recognizing that the change has to begin from within…

But the change can hurt so bad that we just don't want to do it even though we already know that we own the power of change so we must exercise that power and begin with ourselves…

If you change the way you think, you will change the way you behave….If you change the way you behave then you will change the way you live….

And I know it takes courage…but I also know that we are all born with courage but it's when we use it at the right time that makes us courageous.

Changing our minds is the first step in that process….

*How to Get Over It in 30 Days Part II*

**Lesson:** It's like "mind over matter" --- If you don't mind, then it won't matter...The question is "Do you mind?" I think if you want to move towards positive change in your life you should begin to distinguish the things in your life that you should mind vs. the things in your life that shouldn't matter.

Dr. Adair f. White-johnson

# *Here's What I Know:*

Sometimes there are just some things that don't come in that manual called life...

You're left to just figure it out yourself.

But that doesn't mean that you can't ask for help
Or pray for guidance.

It just means that the answer may not be laid out in front of you with a plate, knife, fork, and spoon.

You see, you may get damaged but that doesn't mean you are destroyed

And your heart may feel discouraged but that doesn't mean it is defeated.

Your soul may be a bit tattered, but it's not torn
And those blisters on your toes are not really wounds, they're just throbbing from those painful shoes you may have worn.

Sometimes your vision may appear to be cloudy but you're not really blind
Because when you really push through the pain, those hurtful sights are left behind.

And we know that our faith is often tested
But we also know that if we seek, trust and believe, we are never rejected.

## *How to Get Over It in 30 Days Part II*

And oh, our backs where we carry our burdens are often so sore,
But our inner strength and positive energy that God has given us always allows us to handle just a little more.

All of the pressure and the stress has not broken us yet.
But sometimes our approaches to these rough situations won't let us forget.

There is no one perfect way to live our lives
But remaining in a good frame of mind is step one out of the negativity and strife.

We need to remember not to "borrow worries" and to walk the other way
And to sometimes really get down on our knees to pray

For me, it has made a difference in the ways I cope
And reminds me that even in tragedy there is triumph, in the loss there is a gain, in death there is life and in despair there is hope.

I try to live surrounded by peace and harmony.
Because I know no matter how challenging my life gets my faith, and my God are walking through it right with me.

## Dr. Adair f. White-johnson

***Lesson:*** If faith can move mountains then it can move you too. No matter how bad things get in your life, and you feel like you've lost it all, NEVER, EVER let go of your faith...That's the one thing that no one can take away from you...You can only lose it yourself.

*How to Get Over It in 30 Days Part II*

# *Here's What I Know:*

So as I bring the first day of the rest of my life to a close I am reminded of how blessed and thankful I am.

I could have lost precious time feuding with my Daddy over the little things in life that really don't matter---And not spoken to him for years.

I could have just "thought" about texting him to tell him I loved him, but I didn't --- I actually sent the text messages to let him know how I felt.

I could have pretended that I didn't want his approval of the choices I made, but I wouldn't because his opinion was so very important to me.

I could have faked the laughter at his corny jokes and witty remarks, but I didn't because he was truly funny and intellectually hilarious.

I could have said that I was "too busy" to make the time, energy and effort to see him, spend time with him and listen to him ---But I wanted to be there to hug him and learn from his words of wisdom.

I could have expressed feelings of disappointment when I wanted him to be at every single milestone event of my life and the lives of my children and he couldn't. --- But I knew that I was not the only important person or thing in his life.

## Dr. Adair f. White-johnson

I could have tried to understand why he did some of things he did and the way he did, but I was okay with accepting him for who he really was.

And I could have questioned God's will but I already know that God has a plan for all of us ---We just need to be obedient.

You see, I "coulda, woulda, shoulda" so many things but I simply "didn't" because I knew that I was blessed and thankful for the Daddy I had for the many years that I had him.

Thankful and blessed for his love and commitment to me as a father that never wavered.

Was he perfect? No.
But was he magnificently good? Absolutely.

He gave me what I needed when I needed it.
For this, I am Blessed and Thankful.

When he sent a Thanksgiving meal to my door this evening via a family friend (he knew that my blood pressure was high, I was tired and not feeling well), I knew I was still Blessed and very Thankful.

When he sent the Mormon ladies to my door this evening (they had never been there before) the blessings were still coming my way... When I opened the door all they said was "Good Evening, May we pray with you?" and I knew my Daddy sent them to me.

*How to Get Over It in 30 Days Part II*

Blessings and Thanks.

And when the invitations began pouring in for the Johnson Tribe to share Thanksgiving feasts with other families I knew he was blessing me with the nourishment of the body and soul that I need.

Yes, Daddy was still giving me what I needed when I needed it.

So on this Thanksgiving eve, remember to recognize the things that you are truly blessed with and should be Thankful for.

***Lesson:*** Don't thrive on what you "coulda, shoulda, woulda" done but instead embrace what you can and will do…There are no regrets this way. Blessings and Thanks.

Dr. Adair f. White-johnson

## *"I Won't Forgive..."*

One of the hardest things that I've I had to do in my life was to forgive someone who hurt me.

Someone who hurt me to the core...
Who lit a flame of pain in my spirit and lit a match to my soul?

My heart was on fire because of how I was treated and how badly I was hurting because of this person.

I remember that I couldn't eat...I would raise the fork to my mouth, open my mouth, put the food in my mouth and then couldn't chew.

I felt that I had no energy to eat because all of my energy had been saturated and drained with the hurt.

And "that person" did it to me.

I couldn't sleep...tossing and turning for many nights trying to make the memory of that person disappear and devising ways to get back at them...

> To make them hurt as I hurt...
> To feel as I did.
> To know heartache as I was feeling it...

Yes, I had it bad...I hurt so much so how could I even begin to Get Over It! and begin to forgive that person?

## How to Get Over It in 30 Days Part II

I began by first forgiving myself for allowing me to be in that situation...

There were signs, but I chose not to read them.

Yes, I saw the signs but I made the decision not to read them.
I had to forgive myself for making poor decisions.

I also learned that I wouldn't be able to forgive anyone or anything if I didn't strengthen my faith in God.

That if I didn't believe in his ultimate power to lead me through the pain then, I would never be able to forgive truly.

So I began to lean consistently on my shield of faith more frequently and depend on my prayers being answered for that much-needed strength.

After that, I began allowing myself to heal and then forgiving myself for getting into that situation in the first place.

Only by first healing myself was I able to begin the process of forgiving the other person.

You see, I was no longer angry, hurt and confused. My heart now pumped at a normal pace when I thought of that person and situation.

I knew that forgiving them was a process, and it began by praying for them.
Wrapping them in my prayers daily and asking God to inject my spirit with more compassion and understanding.

Forgiving them was the final step in my own healing process, and I knew that the only way for me to truly move forward and to Get Over It! was to forgive them.

Walking that long, uncomfortable road of forgiveness is challenging but required if we want to heal our inner pain.

It's needed if we want to free ourselves from the jail of hurt that we feel we've been sentenced to.

It's required to liberate ourselves from the emotional enslavement to the mistakes of the past.

We have to write our own proclamation of freedom through the forgiveness of others...

This is the only way to 100% let them go.

And, it's the heart of what it means to be a Christian.

Yes, I know that it's hard to forgive others, and it does take time, energy, and efforts that we think we don't have, but it is necessary.

## *How to Get Over It in 30 Days Part II*

If we don't then the hurt never really goes away...
It emerges each time we see a person who hurt us and every time we think about the situation.

You can't put Band-Aids on gunshot wounds and expect it to heal.
All it will do is become infected and compromise the rest of your body.
It will fester and eventually release toxins that can stagnate your personal growth.

So you have go in and do the surgery on that wound and then stitch it up so you can fully heal...
Forgiving others is that surgery, and you'll need it to move forward in your life and your relationships with others.

I did it.

I performed surgeries in my life...not once or twice but numerous times...

I needed to.<br>
I had to.<br>
So I did.

It was the only way for me to Get Over It! so I could live again...

Forgiveness is hard but living in a world of heartache, and inner pain is harder...Choose to forgive.

## Dr. Adair f. White-johnson

***Lesson:*** If you don't forgive those who may have hurt you then you are sentencing yourself to a jail filled with anger, resentment, and hurt...There's no "get out jail free card" for this kind of pain. Learn to let it go and begin the process of forgiveness.

*How to Get Over It in 30 Days Part II*

# "You Can't Afford Me!"

There are times in my life when I am "richer" because I am "poorer."

It's during these times that I don't have as much money that I want/need that I am reminded that money doesn't have the power to control who I really am...

Although I may not have economic power, I am enriched with the power of God in my life.

I have a positive spirit that is invaluable...
And blessings in my life that are priceless.

I know that my God orders my steps and that if it means walking on the road less traveled then I am enriched with the strength he instilled in me to make the journey.

I don't need money to love myself,
Trust my thoughts,
Remain faithful to the power of my values,
And believe in my ability to accomplish my goals.

My worth is not determined by the salary I earn because no one will ever be able to afford the true value of my existence.

## Dr. Adair f. White-johnson

Just because I experience economic poverty does not mean that I am intellectually and spiritually impoverished.

It just means that I don't have a lot of money.

But that's okay too because I am richer with hope, faith, dreams, love, confidence, courage, diligence, intelligence and competence.

My riches in life don't come from a paycheck...They come from the simple things in life that make the biggest difference in my quality of life...
And that's worth more than any salary.

You see, I already know that money can't buy my happiness at the end of the day because my feelings and my heart are not for sale.

And my spirit cannot be bought with empty souls and faithless deeds.

When I wake up in the morning and look in the mirror, it's not money that I see...
Instead, it's only my own eyes staring back at me.
Not dollar signs.

And when my heart beats it does so I can live...not so I can count money to determine my own worth.

They say "money don't grow on trees" but I also know it don't come out of me either...

It's not who I am...It's just a part of what I do.

## How to Get Over It in 30 Days Part II

So I cannot and will not allow it to define me...
To shape my existence,
Or to determine my self-confidence, self-esteem or self-love...

I'm worth more than that...

For richer...or poorer.

***Lesson:*** Sometimes God strips us down to "nothing" to remind us that we had "everything" all along...And he lets us know that sometimes you are actually "rich" when you feel "poor" because your heart, mind, body, and soul are actually priceless...

*Dr. Adair f. White-johnson*

# *"Let Them Go!!!!"*

If someone is in your life who pulls while you push,
Let them go.

If someone is in your life who makes you feel bad
just so they can feel good,
Let them go.

If there is someone walking around in your world
who puts salt in your sugar, then you just don't need
them in your life.
Let them go.

Although you may not be able to choose who you
love because it's such a raw and natural emotion you
do own the power to choose what you do with that
love and who you allow in your life.

You see, our lives are full of good and bad
relationships but at some point we need to discern
between the two.

At some point, we need clarity about which
relationships work for us and which people are just
toxins in our lives.

Who are these folks who poison us with their words
and venomous actions?

And it's not all about thinking and feeling selfish...
It's just about looking out for oneself.

*How to Get Over It in 30 Days Part II*

Protecting oneself.
Rebuilding oneself.
Recreating oneself.
Improving oneself.
Reclaiming oneself.

You see if we remain caught up in a situation that breeds negativity we will only continue to give birth to hurt and pain that is cloaked in a blanket of shame and doubt.
We will never reach a level of positivity.

If we always bathe in our own dirt of despair and fail to lean on our shields of faith for our support then we will always embrace a source of false Herculean strength.
And then we can only just hope that this will be enough to get us through.

But it won't because it never did.
And it never will.

We have to be willing just to give it up to get over it, get through it and keep it moving.

If they can't be there FOR you then are they really in your life WITH you?
If they cannot say "AMEN" after your prayer then were they even praying at all?

And if you have to question their purpose, integrity and commitment to your excellence do you really need them in your life?

Yes, we all need support to help us become who we dream of becoming, accomplish what we planned to do and claim the victories that belong to us. But we don't have to allow ourselves to be psychologically, emotionally and spiritually assassinated to receive that support.

Let them go.
Give it up.
Get over it.

***Lesson:*** Sometimes we search too hard outside of our "circles" for the things that can hurt us but we must also remember that to turn ourselves "inside out" because we may find the real source of our pain already sharing the same space with us.

*How to Get Over It in 30 Days Part II*

# *Letter to a Friend:*

When are you going to stop abusing yourself?

When will you begin to unlock those shackles that you have chained to your heart in order to love truly and trust again?

So that you can accept yourself as worthy of being loved by someone else?

And when will you sign those emancipation papers to free your mind from the mental enslavement that you sentenced it to?

So you can experience the wonders of the world without a negative attitude?

And how long will it take for you to reposition that mirror on the wall so that when you look at it, stare into your own eyes, you will be able to see the true soul inside?

I need you to begin to learn how to let it all go...to lean on your shield of faith...to allow your spirit to grow.

I need you to understand that it is okay to forgive yourself...that you are the one who can control your own forgiveness and your thoughts...nobody else.

## Dr. Adair f. White-johnson

You have to understand that happiness is not promised to anyone, but the universe is abundant with joy, go ahead and get you some!

And know that for every negative in your life trying to pull you down, there are at least two positives out there to help you Get Over It.
They're just waiting for you...just laying around.

And we all have our darkest days but it's up to you to discover the strength of the sun's rays.

You don't have to keep beating up on yourself, questioning your self-value and your self-worth because you are a child of God...not a curse.

You know that jail of loneliness, despair, and self-doubt that you sentenced yourself to?
 Well, I'm gonna need you to believe that you can be bailed out...that it is not a lifetime sentence and that you deserve to be free too.

Yeah, I get it, and I know it can be hard...But you can't move forward if you don't at least START.

Repeat after me and make this your affirmation today and the next step is to get down on your knees and pray.

"I am. I can. I will. I do. Because I am positive, persistent, powerful and God-filled too."

## *How to Get Over It in 30 Days Part II*

So chin up, keep the faith in your heart, remembering you own the power of change and the ability to make a difference...to have a new start.

You can do this, I believe in you but now you have to believe in yourself to begin the "break-through."

***Lesson:*** It all starts with believing in yourself. For some of us, it comes naturally but others it is a real struggle. Be a true friend and guide those who may be at a crossroad...You never know how much of a difference it will make in their lives.

*Dr. Adair f. White-johnson*

## *Here's What I Know:*

No, my name ain't Dorothy, and I can't click my heels 3x to make my dreams come true.

But, my name is Adair, and I do have my faith in God, the steps he ordered for me and the power of prayer to know what I'm supposed to do.

***Lesson:*** Put your trust in God first and find your shoes later.

*How to Get Over It in 30 Days Part II*

## *Here's What I Know:*

I know that there are some folks out there who disagree with my thoughts and my words.
But that's okay because I don't answer to them.

And there are several, perhaps many, who just don't understand what I do and why I do it.
But that's okay too because I don't need their permission.

And yet there is still another group that remains "on the fence" just trying to figure me out...Not sure what to make of me.
But they can wobble all they want...They are not the shields of faith that I lead on.

You see I first look to my God to strengthen me and fill me up with the courage I'll need to get through.

And I look into the mirror each day to ensure that the reflection staring back at me is tenacious, innovative and sincere so we can stand strong together.

I've created my world of wonders with the people who are a part of it --- my selected family, my selected friends and positive-minded folks...

Since I've done this there really is no need to borrow worries and include those who are not believers.

You see, if we spend every waking hour trying to please others who really don't matter,

## Dr. Adair f. White-johnson

And if we spend quality time responding to situations wrought with negativity,
Then when will we focus on our positive selves?

How can we follow our dreams if we spend so much time combating and reflecting on our nightmares?

At what point do we "Let Go and Let God?"
When do we just "walk away?"

And yes, we may have to walk down a long, uncomfortable road to get where we need to be but we already know that God has ordered our steps anyway.

Some folks just don't want what's right for you and they don't want you to get/receive what is rightfully yours.
They are the "blockers" in your life.

You have to figure how to get around these people who are blocking you from your blessings and your true self.

Figure out how to remove that needle they used to pierce your life with fear and doubt...forcing negativity into your heart like a virus running through your bloodstream.

They must first be numbed and then removed like a cancerous tumor...
But you have to be that surgeon for yourself.

## How to Get Over It in 30 Days Part II

At some point, you've got to cleanse your own wounds so you can begin to heal and move forward.... Learn to doctor your own spirit by anesthetizing it with your faith, belief that you are a child of God and your self-empowerment...

There are always going to be that circle of people who don't believe in you, support your dreams or seek to do you harm....

But you just need to trust and believe in who you are and what you represent, and their actions will begin not to matter in your life.

Remember, man doesn't determine your fate...the steps that God has ordered for you does...

What's for you is already for you...You just have to claim it...

**Lesson:** There are "haters" everywhere...Protect yourself with the love of God. After all, he's the only one that you really answer to.

*Dr. Adair f. White-johnson*

# *"I am not my mistakes."*

I am not my mistakes.
Yes, I make them
But I don't become them.
My first name is not "Mis."and my last name ain't Take."

I'm a lot of things but a "mistake" is not one of them.

And I know that I've made plenty of them, and I probably will make plenty more, but it doesn't mean that I am worthless or useless.

It just makes me human.

You see I already get that I am "so much" but I also understand that I am destined to be "so much more."

And I look at all of my mistakes as the preparation for what's to come...
And lessons to strengthen me for my end result.

My mistakes are not sentences to stupidity.
Or commitments to failure.

They represent resiliency in the raw...
Showing that I have the tenacity to get up and Get Over It! and get ready to try it again in a different way.

The roots of my mistakes are infused in my ability to find my right path in life, encourage my aspirations and cultivate my dreams.

## *How to Get Over It in 30 Days Part II*

You can't find mistakes in my heart because they are not born there; they simply emerge from something right gone wrong...

My mistakes in life don't define me, but they can strengthen my core and distinguish any negative actions from the positives in my daily existence.

I know that I will continue to make mistakes...some bigger than others, but it is my perspective and my plan of redemption that will make a difference in my spiritual, emotional and intellectual growth.

I won't allow my mistakes to divert my hope or stagnate my steps to achievement.

I can't allow my mistakes to limit my possibilities and disable my abilities.

And I don't allow my mistakes to diminish my agency from my own liberation.

So know that when I stumble and fall, the plan is for me to get back up again...Not to wallow in the pain and misery of a temporary setback.

Know that because of my mistakes I am better, stronger and ready to try it again...

I'm not going to dwell over what I did wrong or how it made me feel...I won't allow a mistake to determine my ultimate fate.

## Dr. Adair f. White-johnson

I am empowered with the knowledge that God is on my side and that these are simply the steps he has ordered for me...I am following the path he created just for me.

And even if I make mistakes along the way, I am still a child of God.

> Yes, I get it.
> I understand it.
> I know it.
> I live it.
> But I'm not "it."
> I am not my mistakes.

And you aren't either.
Remember that.

***Lesson:*** We all make mistakes, but it's how we handle them that makes a difference in our lives...

*How to Get Over It in 30 Days Part II*

## *"God is Tryin' to Tell you Something..."*

Sometimes I think that we just don't listen to the Word that God places in our heart and in our lives. Instead, we spend too much time trying to figure it all out ourselves.

We want what we want when we want it, so we ignore the signs that God has placed in our lives to provide answers to our questions and give direction to our dreams.

I am not afraid to use my own life as an example for you to show that it can happen to all of us...

Many of you already know how challenging 2014 has been for me emotionally since the unfortunate, untimely and sudden death of my beloved father last November. But what many of you do not know about is the depth of despair that defined my life for the immediate six months following Daddy's death.

You see, during this time my life was stripped down to the bare essentials of life...I operated at a loss emotionally, physically, psychologically and financially. Life basically "sucked" across the board for me and didn't quite understand why and how everything could "hit" me at the same time.

I questioned God everyday while begging and pleading for his grace and mercy to make things better. I thought I was listening to his Word when I would create action plans to move towards change. I knew that I leaned on my shield of Faith to simply allow me to rise out of bed daily to face all of the problems. And somehow I thought that just because I was a "believer" that everything would be "fixed" on my terms.

Wrong.

See, I was travelling on the right path that God had revealed to me, I was taking the right steps that he ordered for me but I didn't listen to the Word that he sent to me.

I didn't hear him when he said "Be still."
I wasn't paying attention when he said "All is well."
I couldn't find the volume button when he said "Trust and Believe."
And I released the "pause" button while he was speaking about "Obedience."

Instead, I focused on making everything and everybody around me "okay."
I tried to fix it all myself while pretending that I was listening to God.

Wrong Again.

My God has been here all the while….Tryin' to tell me something.
Tryin' to tell me what I needed to hear.

## *How to Get Over It in 30 Days Part II*

If only I would listen.
How many of you are listening to His Word?
How many of you are hearing what he is saying to you?
Really hearing?

You see, listening to what God is trying to tell you requires your undivided attention and obedience.

It is more than just nodding your head and agreeing---
It requires you to "Be Still" so that you can see the gifts that he has shared in your life.

So what if you no longer have the same job because of company workforce reductions? You now have the gift to choose your next career!

So what if your heart is so broken you can't find all the pieces again? You own the gift of allowing someone else to love you!

So what if your spirit feels empty because you think you are missing a piece of it? You now have the gift of filling it with God's presence!

And so what if you are afraid of what tomorrow may bring. You now have the gift of learning how just to enjoy living in the moments of today.

See, I've learned that during this time of heartache and challenge my God was trying to tell me all along that I really needed to "Let Go and Let God."

## Dr. Adair f. White-johnson

He was trying to tell me that everything was already alright because I was traveling along the path he created for me, and he knows which direction I am headed.

He said that he never promised that my path would be a straight path…that there wouldn't be hills to climb, bushes to move out of the way and ditches that I may fall into while traveling. But he said he knew that I would always live in my purpose.

My God, was telling me that despite and in spite of it all, my life was a good life…A thankful life and blessed life.

I know that sometimes we get caught up in things going on around us that we lose connection of things going on inside of us. We stop trusting and believing in the voice that God has whispering in our hearts and our heads and begin to put our faith in what we can do and what others say. But that won't work.

We have to listen.

We have to hear what God is trying to tell us --- that we may "bend but we never break," that we may be "damaged but never destroyed" and that we be those foot soldiers emerging from the trenches but our Faith is really our weapon of mass destruction.

We just have to listen.
We just have to believe.
Because God is ALWAYS "tryin'" to tell us something…..

*How to Get Over It in 30 Days Part II*

## *Here's What I Know:*

Sometimes all you have to "ask" and you will "receive."

I remember really wanting a pair of shoes that I knew I didn't have the "extra" money to buy. I watched these shoes for several months...I would often put them in my online shopping cart but never made it to the checkout. I then watched as they went on sale, and the inventory decreased...

Oh noooo!!!! They won't have my size when I am ready to buy!

A couple of months later and the shoes were still not quite in my budget but at 70% off I knew this would be my last chance to buy them...
But how would I do this? How could I make it work?

I discovered that all I had to do all along was to "ask."

Now I'm not talking about asking God for help or praying to Jesus for a "blessing" to buy them.
I'm saying that sometimes we just need to ask for help from the people that love us.
This extends beyond my desire for a pair of shoes – it applies to our entire lives.

Sometimes we just have to let people help us.
We have to let them love us.
We have to let them do things for us that will make us happy.

## Dr. Adair f. White-johnson

For me, I've struggled with allowing others to help me. As with many of you I suffer from the "Superwoman Syndrome."

You know the disease that makes you believe that you can be all things to all people all the time?
The one that forces you to be the last one asleep but the first one awake each day to ensure that the household runs smoothly?

You know the woman who is the "go-to lady" which fixes all the problems of everyone, but often forgets about herself?

Sound familiar?
Well, that's me.
Well, I should say that "used to be me."
But I've learned that it is okay to accept love and help from others. It doesn't mean that I am a loser or a quitter.
It just means that I need help.

I've learned that sometimes by letting others help me they are helping themselves and in turn that makes me feel good.

You see, sometimes I think we overburden ourselves with feelings of Omnipotence--- as though we can do it all.

We forget that there is only one God, and only he is invincible and can conquer the world.

## How to Get Over It in 30 Days Part II

We get caught up in the human struggle for significance and won't allow ourselves to accept that we cannot do it all.
That we need help.
And then we are afraid to ask for the help.

We let our Fear paralyze our Faith, and we begin to think that if we are not the lone soldier emerging from the trenches then we are not warriors....

Wrong.

We need to let others be a part of our process...a part of our pain and a part of our progress.

We need to let them love us. Help us.

And sometimes they need to love us the best way they know how...

Just because you need something, or someone doesn't mean that you are "needy."

Just because you need help doesn't mean that you are "helpless."

And just because you may depend on receiving help to accomplish something does not make you a "dependent."

Although we own the power of change, that doesn't mean that we have to change it alone.

## Dr. Adair f. White-johnson

Sometimes we just have to accept that we need someone to help us.
And then we just have to ask.

Amazing, after months of pondering about this particular pair of shoes a "light bulb" went off in my head, and I realized how I could solve this "problem."

I simply had to ask for help.

Now some of you are probably saying that this is so trivial, and if I couldn't afford the shoes then, I probably shouldn't get them anyway…
I get that. I understand that. And I know that.

But my point is that if I couldn't find the "strength" to ask for help just for a pair of shoes then how would I find the "strength" to ask for help with more significant things in my life? How would I ever begin to let go of some of the perceived power I thought I needed? How would I learn to "let go" of some of the "pseudo" control?

Hmmmmm….

I learned I had to start somewhere…
And for me, it began with the shoes.

Knowing that it was okay to ask for help when I needed it was a big step and transition for me, and I lifted many burdens from my shoulders over the years.

I now let people love me.
I now let people help me.

And I now "Let Go and Let God" because I know I cannot do it alone…

***Lesson:*** This story is greater than a pair of shoes that I wanted…It was about learning to ask for help when I needed it. And to accept help when it is offered. It was about learning to let others love you. Learning to let others help you. And still knowing that your pride, dignity and faith are all still intact. You lose nothing. And you gain everything. Help. Ask for it.

Dr. Adair f. White-johnson

## *Here's What I Know:*

You are not stronger than God.

No matter how hard you try to make things go in the direction you want them to, God's will always prevail.

You may climb many mountains during your life but God is always waiting for you on the other side because he has pushed all the sharp rocks out of your way and he has passed directly through the actual core of those mountains.

You may feel victorious because you have won many battles in your life, but God provided the artillery you used to win, and he is a champion and always the King.

You may stand courageous by claiming triumph thru tragedy, but it was God's shoulders that you stood on for the strength and the tenacity you used to pull yourself through it all.

And you may be satisfied with accepting life "as is" but it was God who ordered your steps and created the life path upon which you travel.

You see although we are already "so much," God is always so much more.

We need to lean continuously on him and his shields of grace, faith, and mercy for guidance.

# How to Get Over It in 30 Days Part II

Know that we are empowered only by his will.
And nourished only by the gifts he has laid on his table for us to feast upon.

We never limit our possibilities.
We don't disable our abilities.
And we can't predict our future capabilities.

Because we know that our God is the only omnipotent one.

We know that we have to let him do his work and teach us how to do our own.

We must let him lead us as we follow in his footsteps.

And we must live with what he has decided for us -- whether we like it or not.

We are not "special" because we have "gone through" some stuff in our lives...We are simply stronger because of it.

But we are never stronger than God because he has been the one who carried us through it all.

***Lesson***: You never do it alone. You can never be strong without faith in God. You will never be able to "outwit/outsmart" God or even bargain with him to get what you want. It just doesn't work that way. Be accepting and obedient to his Word, and you will find all the strength that you need there.

*Dr. Adair f. White-johnson*

## *Here's What I Know:*

## ***PRAYER CHANGES EVERYTHING.***
## *I am.*
## *I can.*
## *I will.*
## *I do.*

## ABOUT THE AUTHOR

Dr. White-johnson is the author of "Go Hard and Stumble Softly" published in July, 2012 and "Get Over It! 7 Steps to Live Well with Lupus." She is also the author of "Get Over It! How to Bounce Back after Hitting Rock Bottom," "How to Get Over It! in 30 Days" Part I and "Get Over It! How to Bounce Back after Hitting Rock Bottom for Teens." In addition, she has created an award-winning leadership and personal development curriculum and program for teens that is aligned with the national Common Core Standards and the American School Counselor Association National Model Standards. She earned her Ph.D. from the University at Buffalo and holds a master's degree in the counseling field. Dr. White-johnson is married and the mother of five children.

www.ingramcontent.com/pod-product-compliance
Lightning Source LLC
Chambersburg PA
CBHW061646040426
42446CB00010B/1605